BRIGHTER CHILD®

# English & Grammar

Brighter Child®
An imprint of Carson-Dellosa Publishing LLC
P.O. Box 35665
Greensboro, NC 27425  USA

Printed in Minster, OH USA • All rights reserved.    ISBN 0-7696-7624-3

3 4 5 6 7 8 9 10 GLO 14 13 12 11 10                                    180107784

# Table of Contents
## Brighter Child
### English and Grammar
### Grade 4

# Nouns

A noun names a person, place or thing.

**Examples:**

**person** — sister, uncle, boy, woman
**place** — building, city, park, street
**thing** — workbook, cat, candle, bed

**Directions:** Circle the nouns in each sentence. The first one has been done for you.

1. The (dog) ran into the (street.)

2. Please take this book to the librarian.

3. The red apples are in the kitchen.

4. That scarf belongs to the bus driver.

5. Get some blue paper from the office to make a card.

6. Look at the parachute!

7. Autumn leaves are beautiful.

8. The lion roared loudly at the visitors.

**Directions:** Write the nouns you circled in the correct group.

| Persons | Places | Things | |
|---------|--------|--------|---|
| librarian | street | dog | |
| | | | |
| | | | |
| | | | |
| | | | |

# Nouns

**Directions:** Write nouns that name persons.

1. Could you please give this report to my _____ ?

2. The _____ works many long hours to plant crops.

3. I had to help my little _____ when he wrecked his bike yesterday.

**Directions:** Write nouns that name places.

4. I always keep my library books on top of the _____ so I can find them.

5. We enjoyed watching the kites flying high in the _____ .

6. Dad built a nice fire in the _____ to keep us warm.

**Directions:** Write nouns that name things.

7. The little _____ purred softly as I held it.

8. Wouldn't you think a _____ would get tired of carrying its house around all day?

9. The _____ scurried into its hole with the piece of cheese.

10. I can tell by the writing that this _____ is mine.

11. Look at the _____ I made in art.

12. His _____ blew away because of the strong wind.

# Proper Nouns

**Proper nouns** name specific persons, places or things.

**Examples:**

    **person** — Ms. Steiner, Judge Jones, Lt. Raydon

    **place** — Crestview School, California, China

    **thing** — Declaration of Independence, Encyclopedia Britannica

**Directions:** Circle the proper noun in each sentence. Write person, place or thing in the blank. The first one has been done for you.

1. I returned the overdue book to the (Ashland Public Library.)

    <u>Ashland Public Library</u>      place

2. Our new principal is Mrs. Denes.

    _____      _____

3. We enjoyed shopping at Brookland Mall.

    _____      _____

4. Did you finish your report on *Charlotte's Web*?

    _____      _____

5. The new student in our class lives on Reed Road.

    _____      _____

6. Mr. Wilkes said he likes his new job.

    _____      _____

7. How do you get to Millsboro from here?

    _____      _____

# Proper Nouns: Capitalization

Proper nouns always begin with a capital letter.

**Examples:**

Monday

Texas

Karen

Mr. Logan

Hamburger Avenue

Rover

**Directions:** Cross out the lower-case letters at the beginning of the proper nouns. Write capital letters above them. The first one has been done for you

1. My teddy bear's name is C̶ocoa.

2. ms. bernhard does an excellent job at crestview elementary school.

3. emily, elizabeth and megan live on main street.

4. I am sure our teacher said the book report is due on monday.

5. I believe you can find lake street if you turn left at the next light.

6. Will your family be able join our family for dinner at burger barn?

7. The weather forecasters think the storm will hit the coast of louisiana friday afternoon.

8. My family went to washington, d.c. this summer.

9. Remember, we don't have school on tuesday because of the teachers' meeting.

10. Who do you think will win the game, the cougars or the arrows?

# Pronouns

A **pronoun** is a word that takes the place of a noun in a sentence.

**Examples:**

> I, my, mine, me
>
> we, our, ours, us
>
> you, your, yours
>
> he, his, him
>
> she, her, hers
>
> it, its
>
> they, their, theirs, them

**Directions:** Underline the pronouns in each sentence.

1. Bring them to us as soon as you are finished.

2. She has been my best friend for many years.

3. They should be here soon.

4. We enjoyed our trip to the Mustard Museum.

5. Would you be able to help us with the project on Saturday?

6. Our homeroom teacher will not be here tomorrow.

7. My uncle said that he will be leaving soon for Australia.

8. Hurry! Could you please open the door for him?

9. She dropped her gloves when she got off the bus.

10. I can't figure out who the mystery writer is today.

　　　**9**　　　*English and Grammar: Grade 4*

# Nouns and Pronouns

To make a story or report more interesting, pronouns can be substituted for "overused" nouns.

**Example:**

Mother made the beds. Then Mother started the laundry.

The noun **Mother** is used in both sentences. The pronoun **she** could be used in place of **Mother** the second time to make the second sentence more interesting.

**Directions:** Cross out nouns when they appear a second and/or third time. Write a pronoun that could be used instead. The first one has been done for you.

**we**  1. My friends and I like to go ice skating in the winter. ~~My friends and I~~ usually fall down a lot, but ~~my friends and~~ I have fun!

_____ 2. All the children in the fourth-grade class next to us must have been having a party. All the children were very loud. All the children were happy it was Friday.

_____ 3. I try to help my father with work around the house on the weekends. My father works many hours during the week and would not be able to get everything done.

_____ 4. Can I share my birthday treat with the secretary and the principal? The secretary and the principal could probably use a snack right now!

_____ 5. I know Mr. Jones needs a copy of this history report. Please take it to Mr. Jones when you finish.

# Subjects and Predicates

The **subject** tells who or what the sentence is about. The **predicate** tells what the subject does, did, is doing or will do. A complete sentence must have a subject and a predicate.

**Examples:**

| Subject | Predicate |
|---|---|
| Sharon | writes to her grandmother every week. |
| The horse | ran around the track quickly. |
| My mom's car | is bright green. |
| Denise | will be here after lunch. |

**Directions:** Circle the subject of each sentence. Underline the predicate.

1. My sister is a very happy person.

2. I wish we had more holidays in the year.

3. Laura is one of the nicest girls in our class.

4. John is fun to have as a friend.

5. The rain nearly ruined our picnic!

6. My birthday present was exactly what I wanted.

7. Your bicycle is parked beside my skateboard.

8. The printer will need to be filled with paper before you use it.

9. Six dogs chased my cat home yesterday!

10. Anthony likes to read anything he can get his hands on.

11. Twelve students signed up for the dance committee.

12. Your teacher seems to be a reasonable person.

# Subjects and Predicates

**Directions:** Write subjects to complete the following sentences.

1. _____ went to school last Wednesday.

2. _____ did not understand the joke.

3. _____ barked so loudly that no one could sleep a wink.

4. _____ felt unhappy when the ball game was rained out.

5. _____ wonder what happened at the end of the book.

6. _____ jumped for joy when she won the contest.

**Directions:** Write predicates to complete the following sentences.

7. Everyone _____.

8. Dogs _____.

9. I _____.

10. Justin _____.

11. Jokes _____.

12. Twelve people _____.

# Subjects and Predicates

A **sentence** is a group of words that expresses a complete thought. It must have at least one subject and one verb.

**Examples:**

**Sentence:** John felt tired and went to bed early.

**Not a sentence:** Went to bed early.

**Directions:** Write **S** if the group of words is a complete sentence. Write **NS** if the group of words is not a sentence.

_____ 1. Which one of you?

_____ 2. We're happy for the family.

_____ 3. We enjoyed the program very much.

_____ 4. Felt left out and lonely afterwards.

_____ 5. Everyone said it was the best party ever!

_____ 6. No one knows better than I what the problem is.

_____ 7. Seventeen of us!

_____ 8. Quickly before they.

_____ 9. Squirrels are lively animals.

_____ 10. Not many people believe it really happened.

_____ 11. Certainly, we enjoyed ourselves.

_____ 12. Tuned her out.

# Compound Subjects

A **compound subject** is a subject with two parts joined by the word **and** or another conjunction. Compound subjects share the same predicate.

**Example:**

Her shoes were covered with mud. Her ankles were covered with mud, too.

**Compound subject:** Her shoes and ankles were covered with mud.

The predicate in both sentences is **were covered with mud**.

**Directions:** Combine each pair of sentences into one sentence with a compound subject.

1. Bill sneezed. Kassie sneezed.

_____

2. Kristin made cookies. Joey made cookies.

_____

3. Fruit flies are insects. Ladybugs are insects.

_____

4. The girls are planning a dance. The boys are planning a dance.

_____

5. Our dog ran after the ducks. Our cat ran after the ducks.

_____

6. Joshua got lost in the parking lot. Daniel got lost in the parking lot.

_____

# Compound Predicates

A **compound predicate** is a predicate with two parts joined by the word **and** or another conjunction. Compound predicates share the same subject.

**Example:** The baby grabbed the ball. The baby threw the ball.

**Compound predicate:** The baby grabbed the ball and threw it.
The subject in both sentences is **the baby**.

**Directions:** Combine each pair of sentences into one sentence to make a compound predicate.

1. Leah jumped on her bike. Leah rode around the block.

   _____

2. Father rolled out the pie crust. Father put the pie crust in the pan.

   _____

3. Anthony slipped on the snow. Anthony nearly fell down.

   _____

4. My friend lives in a green house. My friend rides a red bicycle.

   _____

5. I opened the magazine. I began to read it quietly.

   _____

6. My father bought a new plaid shirt. My father wore his new red tie.

   _____

# Intransitive Verbs

An **intransitive verb** is a verb that can stand alone in the predicate because its meaning is complete.

**Examples:**

> He **works**.
> They **sleep**.
> The dog **ran**.

Other words are not needed after the intransitive verb to make the sentences complete. If more words are added to the sentence, the verbs would still be intransitive because the sentence could stand alone without additional words.

**Example:**

> The noisy concert ended early.
> **Ended** is still an intransitive verb in this sentence.

**Directions:** Underline the intransitive verb in each sentence.

1. The soccer ball bounced out of bounds.

2. Many autumn leaves fell overnight.

3. Our teacher helped at the band concert yesterday.

4. The small, brown puppy whimpered all night.

5. The school band marched across the field.

6. The cat scratched at the door until dark.

7. The fireworks boomed for hours.

8. The school bus arrived late.

9. A few children cried for their mothers.

10. That feather tickles!

11. Grandfather Wade's barn burned last night.

12. The car tires squealed loudly.

13. The audience laughed at the comedian's jokes.

14. The artist painted in the loft studio.

# Transitive Verbs

A **transitive verb** needs a direct object to complete its meaning. A **direct object** is the word or words that come after a transitive verb to complete its meaning.

**Examples:**

Tim **is** taking dance lessons.

He **did** a dance.

The dance **was** a gig.

**Is**, **did** and **was** are transitive verbs. They must have one or more words after them to complete their meanings.

**Example:**

The bird **found its nest**.

The words **its nest** are needed after the transitive verb **found** to make the sentence complete.

**Directions:** Underline the transitive verb in each sentence.

1. The computer made a strange sound.

2. Last night's thunderstorm ruined our sand castles.

3. Aunt Jean raised tomatoes in her garden.

4. Brad accepted the award at the dinner last night.

5. Dad saw us outside his window.

6. The students in Home Economics baked delicious brownies.

7. We had a lot of homework.

8. He will replace the dead battery.

9. Everyone saw the special on television last night.

10. My dog chased the cat.

11. Morgan saw the kites flying high in the sky.

12. We enjoyed the museum trip.

# Intransitive and Transitive Verbs

**Directions:** Write a **T** in the blanks by the sentences that have a transitive verb. Write an **I** in the blanks by the sentences that have an intransitive verb.

_____ 1. The story was a mystery.

_____ 2. The people cheered loudly.

_____ 3. The neighbor's dog barked yesterday.

_____ 4. We missed her birthday completely.

_____ 5. The lion roared.

_____ 6. Together, we sang many songs.

_____ 7. Elizabeth sharpened her pencil.

_____ 8. She visited New York City last summer.

_____ 9. The kitten cried for several hours.

_____10. Gina arrived late for school.

_____ 11. Did anyone cry when the mayor left?

_____ 12. The thunder boomed loudly.

# Verbs: Present, Past and Future Tense

The **present tense** of a verb tells what is happening now.

**Examples:**

> I **am** happy.
> I **run** fast.

The **past tense** of a verb tells what has already happened.

**Examples:**

> I **was** happy.
> I **ran** fast.

The **future tense** of a verb refers to what is going to happen. The word **will** usually comes before the future tense of a verb.

**Examples:**

> I **will be** happy.
> I **will run** fast.

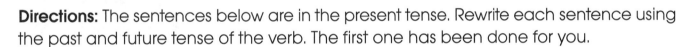

**Directions:** The sentences below are in the present tense. Rewrite each sentence using the past and future tense of the verb. The first one has been done for you.

1. I think of you as my best friend.
   I thought of you as my best friend.
   I will think of you as my best friend.

2. I hear you coming up the steps.
   _____
   _____

3. I rush every morning to get ready for school.
   _____
   _____

4. I bake brownies every Saturday.
   _____
   _____

# Verbs: Present, Past and Future Tense

**Directions:** Read the following sentences. Write **PRES** if the sentence is in present tense. Write **PAST** if the sentence is in past tense. Write **FUT** if the sentence is in future tense. The first one has been done for you.

_FUT_ 1. I will be thrilled to accept the award.

_____ 2. Will you go with me to the dentist?

_____ 3. I thought he looked familiar!

_____ 4. They ate every single slice of pizza.

_____ 5. I run myself ragged sometimes.

_____ 6. Do you think this project is worthwhile?

_____ 7. No one has been able to repair the broken plate.

_____ 8. Thoughtful gifts are always appreciated.

_____ 9. I like the way he sang!

_____ 10. With a voice like that, he will go a long way.

_____ 11. It's my fondest hope that they visit soon.

_____ 12. I wanted that coat very much.

_____ 13. She'll be happy to take your place.

_____ 14. Everyone thinks the test will be a breeze.

_____ 15. Collecting stamps is her favorite hobby.

# Adding "ed" to Make Verbs Past Tense

To make many verbs past tense, add **ed**.

**Examples:**

cook + ed = cooked    wish + ed = wished    play + ed = played

When a verb ends in a **silent e**, drop the **e** and add **ed**.

**Examples:**

hope + ed = hoped    hate + ed = hated

When a verb ends in **y** after a consonant, change the **y** to **i** and add **ed**.

**Examples:**

hurry + ed = hurried    marry + ed = married

When a verb ends in a single consonant after a single short vowel, double the final consonant before adding **ed**.

**Examples:**

stop + ed = stopped    hop + ed = hopped

**Directions:** Rewrite the present tense of the verb correctly. The first one has been done for you.

1. call _____called_____

2. copy _____

3. frown _____

4. smile _____

5. live _____

6. talk _____

7. name _____

8. list _____

9. spy _____

10. phone _____

11. reply _____

12. top _____

13. clean _____

14. scream _____

15. clap _____

16. mop _____

17. soap _____

18. choke _____

19. scurry _____

20. drop _____

# Verbs With "ed"

**Directions:** All the sentences below need a **verb + ed**. Write a word from the box to complete each sentence.

| | | | |
|---|---|---|---|
| talked | watched | served | wagged |
| picked | shared | typed | washed |
| knocked | laughed | bothered | |

1. She _____ on the phone for at least 1 hour.

2. He _____ the vegetables while I prepared the broth for the soup.

3. We never _____ as hard as we did at that clown!

4. Each boy in the class _____ a story about what he had done over the summer.

5. Father _____ the popcorn while Mother put the movie in the VCR.

6. I know that noise _____ you last night.

7. The dog's tail _____ so hard it _____ over the picture on the table.

8. Do you know who _____ the flowers?

9. She carefully _____ her report for health class on the computer.

10. The whole class _____ as the rockets shot up into the sky.

# Irregular Verbs: Past Tense

**Irregular verbs** change completely in the past tense. Unlike regular verbs, past-tense forms of irregular verbs are not formed by adding **ed**.

**Example:** The past tense of **go** is **went**.

Other verbs change some letters to form the past tense.
**Example:** The past tense of **break** is **broke**.

A **helping verb** helps to tell about the past. **Has**, **have** and **had** are helping verbs used with action verbs to show the action occurred in the past. The past-tense form of the irregular verb sometimes changes when a helping verb is added.

| Present Tense Irregular Verb | Past Tense Irregular Verb | Past Tense Irregular Verb With Helper |
|---|---|---|
| go | went | have/has/had gone |
| see | saw | have/has/had seen |
| do | did | have/has/had done |
| bring | brought | have/has/had brought |
| sing | sang | have/has/had sung |
| drive | drove | have/has/had driven |
| swim | swam | have/has/had swum |
| sleep | slept | have/has/had slept |

**Directions:** Choose four words from the chart. Write one sentence using the past-tense form of the verb without a helping verb. Write another sentence using the past-tense form with a helping verb.

1. _____

   _____

2. _____

   _____

3. _____

   _____

4. _____

   _____

**23** *English and Grammar: Grade 4*

# The Irregular Verb "Be"

**Be** is an irregular verb. The present-tense forms of be are **be**, **am**, **is** and **are**. The past-tense forms of **be** are **was** and **were**.

**Directions:** Write the correct form of **be** in the blanks. The first one has been done for you.

1. I _____ am _____ so happy for you!

2. Jared _____ unfriendly yesterday.

3. English can _____ a lot of fun to learn.

4. They _____ among the nicest people I know.

5. They _____ late yesterday.

6. She promises she _____ going to arrive on time.

7. I _____ nervous right now about the test.

8. If you _____ satisfied now, so am I.

9. He _____ as nice to me last week as I had hoped.

10. He can _____ very gracious.

11. Would you _____ offended if I moved your desk?

12. He _____ watching at the window for me yesterday.

# Verbs: "Was" and "Were"

| Singular | Plural |
|---|---|
| I was | we were |
| you were | you were |
| he, she, it was | they were |

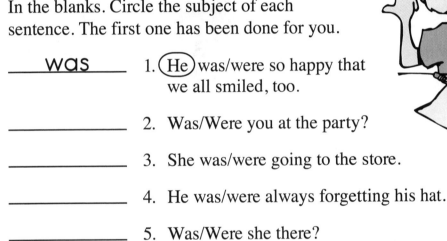

Directions: Write the correct form of the verb In the blanks. Circle the subject of each sentence. The first one has been done for you.

___was___  1. (He) was/were so happy that we all smiled, too.

_____  2. Was/Were you at the party?

_____  3. She was/were going to the store.

_____  4. He was/were always forgetting his hat.

_____  5. Was/Were she there?

_____  6. Was/Were you sure of your answers?

_____  7. She was/were glad to help.

_____  8. They was/were excited.

_____  9. Exactly what was/were you planning to do?

_____  10. It was/were wet outside.

_____  11. They was/were scared by the noise.

_____  12. Was/Were they expected before noon?

_____  13. It was/were too early to get up!

_____  14. She was/were always early.

_____  15. You were/was the first person I asked.

# Verbs: "Went" and "Gone"

The word **went** is used without a helping verb.

**Examples:**

Correct: Susan **went** to the store.

Incorrect: Susan **has went** to the store.

**Gone** is used with a helping verb.

**Examples:**

Correct: Susan **has gone** to the store.

Incorrect: Susan **gone** to the store.

**Directions:** Write **C** in the blank if the verb is used correctly. Draw an **X** in the blank if the verb is not used correctly.

_____C_____ 1. She has gone to my school since last year.

_____ 2. Has not he been gone a long time?

_____ 3. He has went to the same class all year.

_____ 4. I have went to that doctor since I was born.

_____ 5. She is long gone!

_____ 6. Who among us has not gone to get a drink yet?

_____ 7. The class has gone on three field trips this year.

_____ 8. The class went on three field trips this year.

_____ 9. Who has not went to the board with the right answer?

_____ 10. We have not went on our vacation yet.

_____ 11. Who is went for the pizza?

_____ 12. The train has been gone for 2 hours.

_____ 13. The family had gone to the movies.

_____ 14. Have you went to visit the new bookstore?

_____ 15. He has gone on and on about how smart you are!

# Direct Objects

A **direct object** is the word or words that come after a transitive verb to complete its meaning. The direct object answers the question **whom** or **what**.

**Examples:**

Aaron wrote a **letter**.
**Letter** is the direct object. It tells what Aaron wrote.
We heard **Tom**.
**Tom** is the direct object. It tells whom we heard.

**Directions:** Identify the direct object in each sentence. Write it in the blank.

_____ 1. My mother called me.

_____ 2. The baby dropped it.

_____ 3. I met the mayor.

_____ 4. I like you!

_____ 5. No one visited them.

_____ 6. We all heard the cat.

_____ 7. Jessica saw the stars.

_____ 8. She needs a nap.

_____ 9. The dog chewed the bone.

_____ 10. He hugged the doll.

_____ 11. I sold the radio.

_____ 12. Douglas ate the banana.

_____ 13. We finally found the house.

# Indirect Objects

An **indirect object** is the word or words that come between the verb and the direct object. Indirect objects tells **to whom** or **what** or **for whom** or **what** something is done.

**Examples:**

He read **me** a funny story.

**Me** is the indirect object. It tells to whom something (reading a story) was done.

She told her **mother** the truth.

**Mother** is the indirect object. It tells to whom something (telling the truth) was done.

**Directions:** Identify the indirect object in each sentence. Write it in the blank.

1. The coach gave Bill a trophy. _____

2. He cooked me a wonderful meal. _____

3. She told Maria her secret. _____

4. Someone gave my mother a gift. _____

5. The class gave the principal a new flag for the cafeteria. _____

6. The restaurant pays the waiter a good salary. _____

7. You should tell your dad the truth. _____

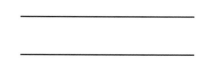

8. She sent her son a plane ticket. _____

9. The waiter served the patron a salad. _____

10. Grandma gave the baby a kiss. _____

11. I sold Steve some cookies. _____

12. He told us six jokes. _____

13. She brought the boy a sucker. _____

# Direct and Indirect Objects

**Example:** Sharon told <u>Jennifer</u> a funny (story.)

Jennifer is the indirect object. It tells **to whom** Sharon told the story. Story is the direct object. It tells **what** Sharon told.

**Directions:** Circle the direct object in each sentence. Underline the indirect object.

1. The teacher gave the class a test.

2. Josh brought Elizabeth the book.

3. Someone left the cat a present.

4. The poet read David all his poems.

5. My big brother handed me the ticket.

6. Luke told everyone the secret.

7. Jason handed his dad the newspaper.

8. Mother bought Jack a suitcase.

9. They cooked us an excellent dinner.

10. I loaned Jonathan my bike.

11. She threw him a curve ball.

12. You tell Dad the truth!

# Adverbs

**Adverbs** are words that tell when, where or how.

**Adverbs of time** tell when.

**Example:**

The train left yesterday.

**Yesterday** is an adverb of time. It tells when the train left.

**Adverbs of place** tell where.

**Example:**

The girl walked away.

**Away** is an adverb of place. It tells where the girl walked.

**Adverbs of manner** tell how.

**Example:**

The boy walked quickly.

**Quickly** is an adverb of manner. It tells how the boy walked.

**Directions:** Write the adverb for each sentence in the first blank. In the second blank, write whether it is an adverb of time, place or manner. The first one has been done for you.

1. The family ate downstairs.     <u>downstairs</u>     <u>place</u>

2. The relatives laughed loudly. _____ _____

3. We will finish tomorrow. _____ _____

4. The snowstorm will stop soon. _____ _____

5. She sings beautifully! _____ _____

6. The baby slept soundly. _____ _____

7. The elevator stopped suddenly. _____ _____

8. Does the plane leave today? _____ _____

9. The phone call came yesterday. _____ _____

10. She ran outside. _____ _____

# Adverbs of Time

**Directions:** Choose a word or group of words from the box to complete each sentence. Make sure the adverb you choose makes sense with the rest of the sentence.

| | |
|---|---|
| in 2 weeks | last winter |
| next week | at the end of the day |
| soon | right now |
| 2 days ago | tonight |

1. We had a surprise birthday party for him _____ .

2. Our science projects are due _____ .

3. My best friend will be moving _____ .

4. Justin and Ronnie need our help _____ !

5. We will find out who the winners are _____ .

6. Can you take me to ball practice _____ ?

7. She said we will be getting a letter _____ .

8. Diane made the quilt _____ .

 *English and Grammar: Grade 4*

# Adverbs of Place

**Directions:** Choose one word from the box to complete each sentence. Make sure the adverb you choose makes sense with the rest of the sentence.

| | | | |
|---|---|---|---|
| inside | upstairs | below | everywhere |
| home | somewhere | outside | there |

1. Each child took a new library book _____ .

2. We looked _____ for his jacket.

3. We will have recess _____ because it is raining.

4. From the top of the mountain we could see the village far

_____ .

5. My sister and I share a bedroom _____ .

6. The teacher warned the children, "You must play with the ball

_____ ."

7. Mother said, "I know that recipe is _____

in this file box!"

8. You can put the chair _____ .

**Name** _____

# Adverbs of Manner

**Directions:** Choose a word from the box to complete each sentence. Make sure the adverb you choose makes sense with the rest of the sentence. One word will be used twice.

| quickly | carefully | loudly | easily | carelessly | slowly |
|---------|-----------|--------|--------|------------|--------|

1. The scouts crossed the old bridge _____ .

2. We watched the turtle move _____ across the yard.

3. Everyone completed the math test _____ .

4. The quarterback scampered _____ down the sideline.

5. The mother _____ cleaned the child's sore knee.

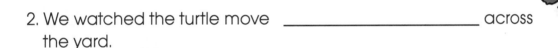

6. The fire was caused by someone _____ tossing a match.

7. The alarm rang _____ while we were eating.

**33**  *English and Grammar: Grade 4*

# Adjectives That Add "er"

The suffix **er** is often added to adjectives to compare two things.

**Example:**

My feet are **large**.

Your feet are **larger** than my feet.

When a one-syllable adjective ends in a single consonant and the vowel is short, double the final consonant before adding **er**. When a word ends in two or more consonants, add **er**.

**Examples:**

big — bigger (single consonant)

bold — bolder (two consonants)

When an adjective ends in **y**, change the **y** to **i** before adding **er**.

**Examples:**

easy — easier

greasy — greasier

breezy — breezier

**Directions:** Use the correct rule to add **er** to the words below. The first one has been done for you.

1. fast      _____faster_____          11. skinny   _____

2. thin      _____         12. fat      _____

3. long      _____         13. poor     _____

4. few       _____         14. juicy    _____

5. ugly      _____         15. early    _____

6. silly     _____         16. clean    _____

7. busy      _____         17. thick    _____

8. grand     _____         18. creamy   _____

9. lean      _____         19. deep     _____

10. young    _____         20. lazy     _____

# Adjectives That Add "est"

The suffix **est** is often added to adjectives to compare more than two things.

**Example:**

My glass is **full**.

Your glass is **fuller**.

His glass is **fullest**.

When a one-syllable adjective ends in a single consonant and the vowel sound is short, you usually double the final consonant before adding est.

**Examples:**

big — biggest (short vowel)

steep — steepest (long vowel)

When an adjective ends in **y**, change the **y** to **i** before adding est.

**Example:**

easy — easiest

**Directions:** Use the correct rule to add **est** to the words below. The first one has been done for you.

1. thin _____thinnest_____     11. quick _____

2. skinny _____     12. trim _____

3. cheap _____     13. silly _____

4. busy _____     14. tall _____

5. loud _____     15. glum _____

6. kind _____     16. red _____

7. dreamy _____     17. happy _____

8. ugly _____     18. high _____

9. pretty _____     19. wet _____

10. early _____     20. clean _____

# Adding "er" and "est" to Adjectives

**Directions:** Circle the correct adjective for each sentence. The first one has been done for you.

1. Of all the students in the gym, her voice was (louder, (loudest)).

2. "I can tell you are (busier, busiest) than I am," he said to the librarian.

3. If you and Carl stand back to back, I can see which one is (taller, tallest).

4. She is the (kinder, kindest) teacher in the whole building.

5. Wow! That is the (bigger, biggest) pumpkin I have ever seen!

6. I believe your flashlight is (brighter, brightest) than mine.

7. "This is the (cleaner, cleanest) your room has been in a long time," Mother said.

8. The leaves on that plant are (prettier, prettiest) than the ones on the window sill.

# Adjectives Preceded by "More"

Most adjectives of two or more syllables are preceded by the word **more** as a way to show comparison between two things.

**Examples:**

Correct: intelligent, more intelligent

Incorrect: intelligenter

Correct: famous, more famous

Incorrect: famouser

**Directions:** Write **more** before the adjectives that fit the rule. Draw an **X** in the blanks of the adjectives that do not fit the rule. To test yourself, say the words aloud using **more** and adding **er** to hear which way sounds correct. The first two have been done for you.

_____X_____ 1. cheap

_____more_____ 2. beautiful

_____ 3. quick

_____ 4. terrible

_____ 5. difficult

_____ 6. interesting

_____ 7. polite

_____ 8. cute

_____ 9. dark

_____ 10. sad

_____ 11. awful

_____ 12. delicious

_____ 13. embarrassing

_____ 14. nice

_____ 15. often

_____ 16. hard

_____ 17. valuable

_____ 18. close

_____ 19. fast

_____ 20. important

# Adjectives Using "er" or "More"

**Directions:** Add the word or words needed in each sentence. The first one has been done for you.

1. I thought the book was _____ than the
   movie. (interesting)

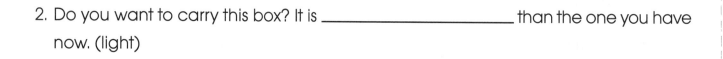

2. Do you want to carry this box? It is _____ than the one you have
   now. (light)

3. I noticed you are moving _____ this morning. Does your ankle
   still bother you? (slow)

4. Thomas Edison is probably _____ for his invention of the
   electric light bulb than of the phonograph. (famous)

5. She stuck out her lower lip and whined, "Your ice-cream cone is
   _____ than mine!" (big)

6. Mom said my room was _____ than it has been in a long time.
   (clean)

# Adjectives Preceded by "Most"

Most adjectives of two or more syllables are preceded by the word **most** as a way to show comparison between more than two things.

**Examples:**

Correct:     intelligent, most intelligent
Incorrect:   intelligentest
Correct:     famous, most famous
Incorrect:   famousest

**Directions:** Read the following groups of sentences. In the last sentence for each group, write the adjective preceded by **most**. The first one has been done for you.

1. My uncle is intelligent.
   My aunt is more intelligent.
   My cousin is the _____ most intelligent _____.

2. I am thankful.
   My brother is more thankful.
   My parents are the _____.

3. Your sister is polite.
   Your brother is more polite.
   You are the _____.

4. The blouse was expensive.
   The sweater was more expensive.
   The coat was the _____.

5. The class was fortunate.
   The teacher was more fortunate.
   The principal was the _____.

6. The cookies were delicious.
   The cake was even more delicious.
   The brownies were the _____.

7. That painting is elaborate.
   The sculpture is more elaborate.
   The finger painting is the _____.

# Adjectives Using "est" or "Most"

**Directions:** Add the word or words needed to complete each sentence. The first one has been done for you.

1. The star over there is the ____brightest____ of all! (bright)

2. "I believe this is the _____ time I have ever had," said Mackenzie. (delightful)

3. That game was the _____ one of the whole year! (exciting)

4. I think this tree has the _____ leaves. (green)

5. We will need the _____ knife you have to cut the face for the jack-o-lantern. (sharp)

6. Everyone agreed that your chocolate chip cookies were the _____ of all. (delicious)

# Adjectives and Adverbs

**Directions**: Write **ADJ** on the line if the bold word is an adjective. Write **ADV** if the bold word is an adverb. The first one has been done for you.

_____ADV_____ 1. That road leads **nowhere**.

_____ 2. The squirrel was **nearby**.

_____ 3. Her **delicious** cookies were all eaten.

_____ 4. Everyone rushed **indoors**.

_____ 5. He **quickly** zipped his jacket.

_____ 6. She hummed a **popular** tune.

_____ 7. Her **sunny** smile warmed my heart.

_____ 8. I hung your coat **there**.

_____ 9. Bring that **here** this minute!

_____ 10. We all walked **back** to school.

_____ 11. The **skinniest** boy ate the most food!

_____ 12. She acts like a **famous** person.

_____ 13. The **silliest** jokes always make me laugh.

_____ 14. She must have parked her car **somewhere**!

_____ 15. Did you take the test **today**?

# "Good" and "Well"

Use the word **good** to describe a noun. Good is an adjective.

**Example:** She is a **good** teacher.

Use the word **well** to tell or ask how something is done or to describe someone's health. Well is an adverb. It describes a verb.

**Example:** She is not feeling **well**.

**Directions:** Write **good** or **well** in the blanks to complete the sentences correctly. The first one has been done for you.

<u>good</u>     1. Our team could use a good/well captain.

_____ 2. The puny kitten doesn't look good/well.

_____ 3. He did his job so good/well that everyone praised him.

_____ 4. Whining isn't a good/well habit.

_____ 5. I might just as good/well do it myself.

_____ 6. She was one of the most well-/good- liked girls at school.

_____ 7. I did the book report as good/well as I could.

_____ 8. The television works very good/well.

_____ 9. You did a good/well job repairing the TV!

_____ 10. Thanks for a job good/well done!

_____ 11. You did a good/well job fixing the computer.

_____ 12. You had better treat your friends good/well.

_____ 13. Can your grandmother hear good/well?

_____ 14. Your brother will be well/good soon.

# "Your" and "You're"

The word **your** shows possession.

**Examples:**

> Is that **your** book?

> I visited **your** class.

The word **you're** is a contraction for **you are**. A **contraction** is two words joined together as one. An apostrophe shows where letters have been left out.

**Examples:**

> You're doing well on that painting.

> If you're going to pass the test, you should study.

**Directions:** Write **your** or **you're** on the blanks to complete the sentences correctly. The first one has been done for you.

__You're__    1. Your/You're the best friend I have!

_____    2. Your/You're going to drop that!

_____    3. Your/You're brother came to see me.

_____    4. Is that your/you're cat?

_____    5. If your/you're going, you'd better hurry!

_____    6. Why are your/you're fingers so red?

_____    7. It's none of your/you're business!

_____    8. Your/You're bike's front tire is low.

_____    9. Your/You're kidding!

_____    10. Have it your/you're way.

_____    11. I thought your/you're report was great!

_____    12. He thinks your/you're wonderful!

_____    13. What is your/you're first choice?

_____    14. What's your/you're opinion?

_____    15. If your/you're going, so am I!

_____    16. Your/You're welcome.

**43**                *English and Grammar: Grade 4*

# "Good" and "Well"; "Your" and "You're"

**Directions:** Choose the correct word for each sentence: **good**, **well**, **your** or **you're**.

1. Are you sure you can see _____ enough to read with the lighting you have?

2. _____ going to need a paint smock when you go to art class tomorrow afternoon.

3. I can see _____ having some trouble. Can I help with that?

4. The music department needs to buy a speaker system that has _____ quality sound.

5. The principal asked, "Where is _____ hall pass?"

6. You must do the job _____ if you expect to keep it.

7. The traffic policeman said, "May I please see _____ driver's license?"

8. The story you wrote for English class was done quite _____ .

9. That radio station you listen to is a _____ one.

10. Let us know if _____ unable to attend the meeting on Saturday.

# "Its" and "It's"

The word **its** shows ownership.

**Examples:**

> **Its** leaves have all turned green.
> **Its** paw was injured.

The word **it's** is a contraction for **it is**.

**Examples:**

> **It's** better to be early than late.
> **It's** not fair!

**Directions:** Write **its** or **it's** to complete the sentences correctly. The first one has been done for you.

_It's_ 1. Its/It's never too late for ice cream!

_____ 2. Its/It's eyes are already open.

_____ 3. Its/It's your turn to wash the dishes!

_____ 4. Its/It's cage was left open.

_____ 5. Its/It's engine was beyond repair.

_____ 6. Its/It's teeth were long and pointed.

_____ 7. Did you see its/it's hind legs?

_____ 8. Why do you think its/it's mine?

_____ 9. Do you think its/it's the right color?

_____ 10. Don't pet its/it's fur too hard!

_____ 11. Its/It's from my Uncle Harry.

_____ 12. Can you tell its/it's a surprise?

_____ 13. Is its/it's stall always this clean?

_____ 14. Its/It's not time to eat yet.

_____ 15. She says its/it's working now.

**45** *English and Grammar: Grade 4*

# "Can" and "May"

The word **can** means am able to or to be able to.

**Examples:**

> I **can** do that for you.
> **Can** you do that for me?

The word **may** means be allowed to or permitted to. May is used to ask or give permission. **May** can also mean **might** or **perhaps**.

**Examples:**

> **May** I be excused?
> You **may** sit here.

**Directions:** Write **can** or **may** on the blanks to complete the sentences correctly. The first one has been done for you.

_May___ 1. Can/May I help you?

_____ 2. He's smart. He can/may do it himself.

_____ 3. When can/may I have my dessert?

_____ 4. I can/may tell you exactly what she said.

_____ 5. He can/may speak French fluently.

_____ 6. You can/may use my pencil.

_____ 7. I can/may be allowed to attend the concert.

_____ 8. It's bright. I can/may see you!

_____ 9. Can/May my friend stay for dinner?

_____ 10. You can/may leave when your report is finished.

_____ 11. I can/may see your point!

_____ 12. She can/may dance well.

_____ 13. Can/May you hear the dog barking?

_____ 14. Can/May you help me button this sweater?

_____ 15. Mother, can/may I go to the movies?

# "Sit" and "Set"

The word **sit** means to rest.

**Examples:**

Please **sit** here!

Will you **sit** by me?

The word **set** means to put or place something.

**Examples:**

**Set** your purse there.

**Set** the dishes on the table.

**Directions:** Write **sit** or **set** to complete the sentences correctly. The first one has been done for you.

| | |
|---|---|
| _____sit_____ | 1. Would you please sit/set down here? |
| _____ | 2. You can sit/set the groceries there. |
| _____ | 3. She sit/set her suitcase in the closet. |
| _____ | 4. He sit/set his watch for half past three. |
| _____ | 5. She's a person who can't sit/set still. |
| _____ | 6. Sit/set the baby on the couch beside me. |
| _____ | 7. Where did you sit/set your new shoes? |
| _____ | 8. They decided to sit/set together during the movie. |
| _____ | 9. Let me sit/set you straight on that! |
| _____ | 10. Instead of swimming, he decided to sit/set in the water. |
| _____ | 11. He sit/set the greasy pan in the sink. |
| _____ | 12. She sit/set the file folder on her desk. |
| _____ | 13. Don't ever sit/set on the refrigerator! |
| _____ | 14. She sit/set the candles on the cake. |
| _____ | 15. Get ready! Get sit/set! Go! |

# "They're," "Their," "There"

The word **they're** is a contraction for **they are**.

**Examples:**

> **They're** our very best friends!
>
> Ask them if **they're** coming over tomorrow.

The word **their** shows ownership.

**Examples:**

> **Their** dog is friendly.
>
> It's **their** bicycle.

The word **there** shows place or direction.

**Examples:**

> Look over **there**.
>
> **There** it is.

**Directions:** Write **they're**, **their** or **there** to complete the sentences correctly. The first one has been done for you.

_There_ 1. They're/Their/There is the sweater I want!

_____ 2. Do you believe they're/their/there stories?

_____ 3. Be they're/their/there by one o'clock.

_____ 4. Were you they're/their/there last night?

_____ 5. I know they're/their/there going to attend.

_____ 6. Have you met they're/their/there mother?

_____ 7. I can go they're/their/there with you.

_____ 8. Do you like they're/their/there new car?

_____ 9. They're/Their/There friendly to everyone.

_____ 10. Did she say they're/their/there ready to go?

_____ 11. She said she'd walk by they're/their/there house.

_____ 12. Is anyone they're/their/there?

_____ 13. I put it right over they're/their/there!

# "This" and "These"

The word **this** is an adjective that refers to things that are near. **This** always describes a singular noun. Singular means one.

**Example:**

I'll buy **this** coat.

(Coat is singular.)

The word **these** is also an adjective that refers to things that are near. **These** always describes a plural noun. A plural refers to more than one thing.

**Example:**

I will buy **these** flowers.

(Flowers is a plural noun.)

**Directions:** Write **this** or **these** to complete the sentences correctly. The first one has been done for you.

___these___ 1. I will take this/these cookies with me.

_____ 2. Do you want this/these seeds?

_____ 3. Did you try this/these nuts?

_____ 4. Do it this/these way!

_____ 5. What do you know about this/these situation?

_____ 6. Did you open this/these doors?

_____ 7. Did you open this/these window?

_____ 8. What is the meaning of this/these letters?

_____ 9. Will you carry this/these books for me?

_____ 10. This/These pans are hot!

_____ 11. Do you think this/these light is too bright?

_____ 12. Are this/these boots yours?

_____ 13. Do you like this/these rainy weather?

# Making Sense of Sentences

A **statement** is a sentence that tells something. It ends with a period (.).

**Example:** Columbus is the capital of Ohio.

A **question** is a sentence that asks something. It ends with a question mark (?).

**Example:** Do you like waffles?

An **exclamation** is a sentence that shows strong feeling.
It ends with an exclamation mark (!).

**Example:** You're the best friend in the world!

A **command** is a sentence that orders someone to do something. It ends with a period or exclamation mark.

**Example:** Shut the door. Watch out for that trunk!

A **request** is a sentence that asks someone to do something. It ends with a period or question mark.

**Example:** Please shut the door.

**Directions:** Write **S** if the sentence makes a statement, **Q** if it asks a question, **E** if it is an exclamation, **C** if it issues a command or **R** if it makes a request. Punctuate each sentence correctly.

_____ 1. Please open your mouth

_____ 2. Will you be going to the party

_____ 3. That's hot

_____ 4. Give me the car keys right now

_____ 5. Do you think she will run fast

_____ 6. It's cold today

_____ 7. You're incredible

_____ 8. Run for your life

_____ 9. Is today the deadline

_____ 10. I turned in my paper early

_____ 11. Call the doctor immediately

_____ 12. Turn around and touch your toes

_____ 13. Be at my house at noon tomorrow

_____ 14. Give me a clue

_____ 15. Can you give me a clue

_____ 16. Please wipe your face

_____ 17. It's time for me to go home

_____ 18. No one believed what she said

_____ 19. Are you interested

_____ 20. He's badly hurt

# Writing Question Sentences

**Directions:** Rewrite each sentence to make it a question. The first one has been done for you. In some cases, the form of the verb must be changed.

1. She slept soundly all day.

   Did she sleep soundly all day?

2. The cookies are hot.

   _____

3. He put the cake in the oven.

   _____

4. She lives in the green house.

   _____

5. He understood my directions.

   _____

6. Jessica ran faster than anyone.

   _____

7. The bus was gone before he arrived.

   _____

8. His car is yellow.

   _____

9. Elizabeth wants some more beans.

   _____

# Conjunctions

Words that join sentences or combine ideas like **and**, **but**, **or**, **because**, **when**, **after** and **so** are called **conjunctions**.

**Examples:**

I played the drums, **and** Sue played the clarinet.
She likes bananas, **but** I do not.
We could play music **or** just enjoy the silence.
I needed the book **because** I had to write a book report.
He gave me the book **when** I asked for it.
I asked her to eat lunch **after** she finished the test.
You wanted my bike **so** you could ride it.

Using different conjunctions can affect the meaning of a sentence.

**Example:**

He gave me the book **when** I asked for it.
He gave me the book **after** I asked for it.

**Directions:** Choose the best conjunction to combine the pairs of sentences. The first one has been done for you.

1. I like my hair curly. Mom likes my hair straight.

I like my hair curly, but Mom likes it straight.

2. I can remember what she looks like. I can't remember her name.

_____

3. We will have to wash the dishes. We won't have clean plates for dinner.

_____

4. The yellow flowers are blooming. The red flowers are not.

_____

5. I like banana cream pie. I like chocolate donuts.

_____

# "And," "But," "Or"

**Directions:** Write **and**, **but** or **or** to complete the sentences.

1. I thought we might try that new hamburger place, _____
   Mom wants to eat at the Spaghetti Shop.

2. We could stay home, _____ would you rather go to the game?

3. She went right home after school, _____ he stopped at the store.

4. Mother held the piece of paneling, _____ Father nailed it in place.

5. She babysat last weekend, _____ her big sister went with her.

6. She likes raisins in her oatmeal, _____ I would rather have mine with
   brown sugar.

7. She was planning on coming over tomorrow, _____ I asked her if she
   could wait until the weekend.

8. Tomato soup with crackers sounds good to me, _____ would you rather
   have vegetable beef soup?

　　　　**53**　　　　*English and Grammar: Grade 4*

# "Because" and "So"

**Directions:** Write **because** or **so** to complete the sentences.

1. She cleaned the paint brushes _____ they would be ready in the morning.

2. Father called home complaining of a sore

   throat _____ Mom stopped by the pharmacy.

3. His bus will be running late _____ it has a flat tire.

4. We all worked together _____ we could get the job done sooner.

5. We took a variety of sandwiches on the picnic _____ we knew not everyone liked cheese and olives with mayonnaise.

6. All the school children were sent home _____ the electricity went off at school.

7. My brother wants us to meet his girlfriend _____ she will be coming to dinner with us on Friday.

8. He forgot to take his umbrella along this morning _____ now his clothes are very wet.

# "When" and "After"

**Directions:** Write **when** or **after** to complete the sentences.

1. I knew we were in trouble _____ I heard the thunder in the distance.

2. We carried the baskets of cherries to the car _____ we were finished picking them.

3. Mother took off her apron _____ I reminded her that our dinner guests would be here any minute.

4. I wondered if we would have school tomorrow _____ I noticed the snow begin to fall.

5. The boys and girls all clapped _____ the magician pulled the colored scarves out of his sleeve.

6. I was startled _____ the phone rang so late last night.

7. You will need to get the film developed _____ you have taken all the pictures.

8. The children began to run _____ the snake started to move!

# Conjunctions

**Directions:** Choose the best conjunction from the box to combine the pairs of sentences. Then rewrite the sentences.

| and | but | or | because | when | after | so |
|-----|-----|-----|---------|------|-------|-----|

1. I like Leah. I like Ben.

_____

2. Should I eat the orange? Should I eat the apple?

_____

3. You will get a reward. You turned in the lost item.

_____

4. I really mean what I say! You had better listen!

_____

5. I like you. You're nice, friendly, helpful and kind.

_____

6. You can have dessert. You ate all your peas.

_____

7. I like your shirt better. You should decide for yourself.

_____

8. We walked out of the building. We heard the fire alarm.

_____

9. I like to sing folk songs. I like to play the guitar.

_____

# Run-On Sentences

A **run-on sentence** occurs when two or more sentences are joined together without punctuation.

**Examples:**

**Run-on sentence**: I lost my way once did you?
**Two sentences with correct punctuation**: I lost my way once. Did you?
**Run-on sentence**: I found the recipe it was not hard to follow.
**Two sentences with correct punctuation**: I found the recipe. It was not hard to follow.

**Directions:** Rewrite the run-on sentences correctly with periods, exclamation points and question marks. The first one has been done for you.

1. Did you take my umbrella I can't find it anywhere!

<u>Did you take my umbrella? I can't find it anywhere!</u>

2. How can you stand that noise I can't!

_____

3. The cookies are gone I see only crumbs.

_____

4. The dogs were barking they were hungry.

_____

5. She is quite ill please call a doctor immediately!

_____

6. The clouds came up we knew the storm would hit soon.

_____

7. You weren't home he stopped by this morning.

_____

# Combining Sentences

Some simple sentences can be easily combined into one sentence.

**Examples:**

  **Simple sentences**: The bird sang. The bird was tiny. The bird was in the tree.
  **Combined sentence**: The tiny bird sang in the tree.

**Directions:** Combine each set of simple sentences into one sentence. The first one has been done for you.

1. The big girls laughed. They were friendly. They helped the little girls.

_The big, friendly girls laughed as they helped the little girls._

2. The dog was hungry. The dog whimpered. The dog looked at its bowl.

_____

3. Be quiet now. I want you to listen. You listen to my joke!

_____

4. I lost my pencil. My pencil was stubby. I lost it on the bus.

_____

5. I see my mother. My mother is walking. My mother is walking down the street.

_____

6. Do you like ice cream? Do you like hot dogs? Do you like mustard?

_____

7. Tell me you'll do it! Tell me you will! Tell me right now!

_____

# Punctuation: Commas

Use a comma to separate the number of the day of a month and the year. Do not use a comma to separate the month and year if no day is given.

**Examples:**

June 14, 1999

June 1999

Use a comma after **yes** or **no** when it is the first word in a sentence.

**Examples:**

Yes, I will do it right now.

No, I don't want any.

**Directions:** Write **C** if the sentence is punctuated correctly. Draw an **X** if the sentence is not punctuated correctly. The first one has been done for you.

__C__ 1. No, I don't plan to attend.

_____ 2. I told them, oh yes, I would go.

_____ 3. Her birthday is March 13, 1995.

_____ 4. He was born in May, 1997.

_____ 5. Yes, of course I like you!

_____ 6. No I will not be there.

_____ 7. They left for vacation on February, 14.

_____ 8. No, today is Monday.

_____ 9. The program was first shown on August 12, 1991.

_____ 10. In September, 2007 how old will you be?

_____ 11. He turned 12 years old on November, 13.

_____ 12. I said no, I will not come no matter what!

_____ 13. Yes, she is a friend of mine.

_____ 14. His birthday is June 12, 1992, and mine is June 12, 1993.

_____ 15. No I would not like more dessert.

     *English and Grammar: Grade 4*

# Punctuation: Commas

Use a comma to separate words in a series. A comma is used after each word in a series but is not needed before the last word. Both ways are correct. In your own writing, be consistent about which style you use.

**Examples:**

> We ate apples, oranges, and pears.
> We ate apples, oranges and pears.

Always use a comma between the name of a city and a state.

**Example:**

> She lives in Fresno, California.
> He lives in Wilmington, Delaware.

**Directions:** Write **C** if the sentence is punctuated correctly. Draw an **X** if the sentence is not punctuated correctly. The first one has been done for you.

___X___ 1. She ordered shoes, dresses and shirts to be sent to her home in Oakland California.

_____ 2. No one knew her pets' names were Fido, Spot and Tiger.

_____ 3. He likes green beans lima beans, and corn on the cob.

_____ 4. Typing paper, pens and pencils are all needed for school.

_____ 5. Send your letters to her in College Park, Maryland.

_____ 6. Orlando Florida is the home of Disney World.

_____ 7. Mickey, Minnie, Goofy and Daisy are all favorites of mine.

_____ 8. Send your letter to her in Reno, Nevada.

_____ 9. Before he lived in New York, City he lived in San Diego, California.

_____ 10. She mailed postcards, and letters to him in Lexington, Kentucky.

_____ 11. Teacups, saucers, napkins, and silverware were piled high.

_____ 12. Can someone give me a ride to Indianapolis, Indiana?

_____ 13. He took a train a car, then a boat to visit his old friend.

_____ 14. Why can't I go to Disney World to see Mickey, and Minnie?

# Punctuation: Quotation Marks

Use quotation marks (" ") before and after the exact words of a speaker.

**Examples:**

I asked Aunt Martha, "How do you feel?"

"I feel awful," Aunt Martha replied.

Do not put quotation marks around words that report what the speaker said.

**Examples:**

Aunt Martha said she felt awful.

I asked Aunt Martha how she felt.

**Directions:** Write **C** if the sentence is punctuated correctly. Draw an **X** if the sentence is not punctuated correctly. The first one has been done for you.

___C___ 1. "I want it right now!" she demanded angrily.

_____ 2 "Do you want it now? I asked."

_____ 3. She said "she felt better" now.

_____ 4. Her exact words were, "I feel much better now!"

_____ 5. "I am so thrilled to be here!" he shouted.

_____ 6. "Yes, I will attend," she replied.

_____ 7. Elizabeth said "she was unhappy."

_____ 8. "I'm unhappy," Elizabeth reported.

_____ 9. "Did you know her mother?" I asked.

_____ 10. I asked "whether you knew her mother."

_____ 11. I wondered, "What will dessert be?"

_____ 12. "Which will it be, salt or pepper?" the waiter asked.

_____ 13. "No, I don't know the answer!" he snapped.

_____ 14. He said "yes he'd take her on the trip.

_____ 15. Be patient, he said. "it will soon be over."

 *English and Grammar: Grade 4*

# Punctuation: Quotation Marks

Use quotation marks around the titles of songs and poems.

**Examples:**

Have you heard "Still Cruising" by the Beach Boys?

"Ode To a Nightingale" is a famous poem.

**Directions:** Write **C** if the sentence is punctuated correctly. Draw an **X** if the sentence is not punctuated correctly. The first one has been done for you.

__C__ 1. Do you know "My Bonnie Lies Over the Ocean"?

_____ 2. We sang The Stars and Stripes Forever" at school.

_____ 3. Her favorite song is "The Eensy Weensy Spider."

_____ 4. Turn the music up when "A Hard Day's "Night comes on!

_____ 5. "Yesterday" was one of Paul McCartney's most famous songs.

_____ 6. "Mary Had a Little Lamb" is a very silly poem!

_____ 7. A song everyone knows is "Happy Birthday."

_____ 8. "Swing Low, Sweet Chariot" was first sung by slaves.

_____ 9. Do you know the words to Home on "the Range"?

_____10. "Hiawatha" is a poem many older people had to memorize.

_____11. "Happy Days Are Here Again! is an upbeat tune.

_____12. Frankie Valli and the Four Seasons sang "Sherry."

_____13. The words to "Rain, Rain" Go Away are easy to learn.

_____14. A slow song I know is called "Summertime."

_____15. Little children like to hear "The Night Before Christmas."

**62**

# Book Titles

All words in the title of a book are underlined. Underlined words also mean italics.

**Examples:**

The Hunt for Red October was a best-seller!
(*The Hunt for Red October*)

Have you read Lost in Space? (*Lost in Space*)

**Directions:** Underline the book titles in these sentences. The first one has been done for you.

1. The Dinosaur Poster Book is for eight year olds.

2. Have you read Lion Dancer by Kate Waters?

3. Baby Dinosaurs and Giant Dinosaurs were both written by Peter Dodson.

4. Have you heard of the book That's What Friends Are For by Carol Adorjan?

5. J.B. Stamper wrote a book called The Totally Terrific Valentine Party Book.

6. The teacher read Almost Ten and a Half aloud to our class.

7. Marrying Off Mom is about a girl who tries to get her widowed mother to start dating.

8. The Snow and The Fire are the second and third books by author Caroline Cooney.

9. The title sounds silly, but Goofbang Value Daze really is the name of a book!

10. A book about space exploration is The Day We Walked on the Moon by George Sullivan.

11. Alice and the Birthday Giant tells about a giant who came to a girl's birthday party.

12. A book about a girl who is sad about her father's death is called Rachel and the Upside Down Heart by Eileen Douglas.

13. Two books about baseball are Baseball Bloopers and Oddball Baseball.

14. Katharine Ross wrote Teenage Mutant Ninja Turtles: The Movie Storybook.

# Book Titles

Capitalize the first and last word of book titles. Capitalize all other words of book titles except short prepositions, such as **of**, **at** and **in**; conjunctions, such as **and**, **or** and **but**; and articles, such as **a**, **an** and **the**.

**Examples:**

Have you read <u>War and Peace</u>?

*Pippi Longstocking in Moscow* is her favorite book.

**Directions:** Underline the book titles. Circle the words that should be capitalized. The first one has been done for you.

1. (murder) in the (blue room) by Elliot Roosevelt

2. growing up in a divided society by Sandra Burnham

3. the corn king and the spring queen by Naomi Mitchison

4. new kids on the block by Grace Catalano

5. best friends don't tell lies by Linda Barr

6. turn your kid into a computer genius by Carole Gerber

7. 50 simple things you can do to save the earth by Earth Works Press

8. garfield goes to waist by Jim Davis

9. the hunt for red october by Tom Clancy

10. fall into darkness by Christopher Pike

11. oh the places you'll go! by Dr. Seuss

12. amy the dancing bear by Carly Simon

13. the great waldo search by Martin Handford

14. the time and space of uncle albert by Russel Stannard

15. true stories about abraham lincoln by Ruth Gross

# Proofreading

**Proofreading** means searching for and correcting errors by carefully reading and rereading what has been written. Use the proofreading marks below when correcting your writing or someone else's.

To insert a word or a punctuation mark that has been left out, use this mark: ∧.
It is called a caret.

     went
**Example:** We∧to the dance together.

To show that a letter should be capitalized, put three lines under it.

**Example:** Mrs. jones drove us to school.
      ≡

To show that a capital letter should be a small or lower-case, draw a diagonal line through it.

**Example:** Mrs. Jones ⱡrove us to school.

To show that a word is spelled incorrectly, draw a horizontal line through it and write the correct spelling above it.

     walrus
**Example:** The ~~wolros~~ is an amazing animal.

**Directions:** Proofread the two paragraphs using the proofreading marks you learned. The author's last name, Towne, is spelled correctly.

### The Modern ark

My book report is on the modern ark by Cecilia Fitzsimmons. The book tells abut 80 of

worlds endangered animals. The book also an arc and animals inside for kids put together.

### Their House

there house is a Great book! The arthur's name is Mary Towne. they're house tells about

a girl name Molly. Molly's Family bys an old house from some people named warren. Then

there big problems begin!

# Proofreading

**Directions:** Proofread the paragraphs, using the proofreading marks you learned. There are seven capitalization errors, three missing words and eleven errors in spelling or word usage.

**Key West**

key West has been tropical paradise ever since Ponce de Leon first saw the set of islands called the keys in 1513. Two famus streets in Key West are named duval and whitehead. You will find the city semetery on Francis Street. The tombstones are funny!

The message on one is, "I told you I was sick!" On sailor's tombston is this mesage his widow: "At lease I no where to find him now."

The cemetery is on 21 akres in the midle of town. The most famous home in key west is that of the authur, Ernest Hemingway. Heminway's home was at 907 whitehead Street. He lived their for 30 years.

# Proofreading

**Directions:** Read more about Key West. Proofread and correct the errors. There are eight errors in capitalization, seven misspelled words, a missing comma and three missing words.

### More About Key West

a good way to lern more about key West is to ride the trolley. Key West has a great troley system. The trolley will take on a tour of the salt ponds. You can also three red brick forts. The troley tour goes by a 110-foot high lighthouse. It is rite in the middle of the city. Key west is the only city with a Lighthouse in the midle of it! It is also the southernmost city in the United States.

If you have time, the new Ship Wreck Museum. Key west was also the hom of former president Harry truman. During his presidency, Trueman spent many vacations on key west.

# Proofreading

**Directions:** Proofread the sentences. Write **C** if the sentence has no errors. Draw an **X** if the sentence contains missing words or other errors. The first one has been done for you.

__C__ 1. The new Ship Wreck Museum in Key West is exciting!

_____ 2. Another thing I liked was the litehouse.

_____ 3. Do you remember Hemingway's address in Key West?

_____ 4. The Key West semetery is on 21 acres of ground.

_____ 5. Ponce de eon discovered Key West.

_____ 6. The cemetery in Key West is on Francis Street.

_____ 7. My favorete tombstone was the sailor's.

_____ 8. His wife wrote the words on it. Remember?

_____ 9. The words said, "at least I know where to find him now!"

_____ 10. That sailor must have been away at sea all the time.

_____ 11. The troley ride around Key West is very interesting.

_____ 12. Do you why it is called Key West?

_____ 13. Can you imagine a lighthouse in the middle of your town?

_____ 14. It's interesting to no that Key West is our southernmost city.

_____ 15. Besides Harry Truman and Hemingway, did other famous people live there?

# Proofreading

**Directions:** Each of the following sentences has a word missing. Use a caret to insert the missing word. The first one has been done for you.

This summer I am
Lake
going to ^ Powell.

Key
1. Have you ever ridden the trolley around ^ West?

2. The Key West lighthouse 110 feet high.

3. Ponce de Leon first the Keys in 1513.

4. Two famous streets in Key West named Duval and Whitehead.

5. The most famous home in Key West that of Ernest Hemingway.

6. The cemetery in Key West on 21 acres.

7. It is located the middle of town.

8. What strange place for a cemetery!

HERE LIES
HARRY
POTTER
1721-1782
HERE LIES
POTTER'S
PIG

9. Many of the tombstones funny!

10. The funniest one has message from a widow of a sailor.

**69** *English and Grammar: Grade 4*

## Page 5

### Nouns

A noun names a person, place or thing.

**Examples:**

**person** — sister, uncle, boy, woman
**place** — building, city, park, street
**thing** — workbook, cat, candle, bed

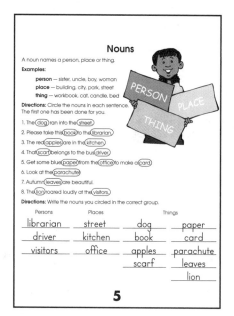

**Directions:** Circle the nouns in each sentence. The first one has been done for you.

1. The (dog) ran into the (street.)
2. Please take this (book) to the (librarian.)
3. The red (apples) are in the (kitchen.)
4. That (scarf) belongs to the bus (driver.)
5. Get some blue (paper) from the (office) to make a (card.)
6. Look at the (parachute.)
7. Autumn (leaves) are beautiful.
8. The (lion) roared loudly at the (visitors.)

**Directions:** Write the nouns you circled in the correct group.

| Persons | Places | Things | |
|---|---|---|---|
| librarian | street | dog | paper |
| driver | kitchen | book | card |
| visitors | office | apples | parachute |
| | | scarf | leaves |
| | | | lion |

**5**

## Page 6

### Nouns

**Directions:** Write nouns that name persons.

1. Could you please give this report to my _____?
2. The _____ works many long hours to plant crops.
3. I had to help my little _____ when he wrecked his bike yesterday.

**Directions:** Write nouns that name places.

4. I always keep my library books on top of the _____ so I can find them.
5. We enjoyed watching the kites fly _____
6. Dad built a nice _____ to keep us warm.

**Directions:** Write nouns that name things.

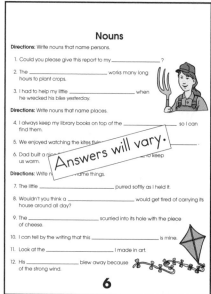

7. The little _____ purred softly as I held it.
8. Wouldn't you think a _____ would get tired of carrying its house around all day?
9. The _____ scurried into its hole with the piece of cheese.
10. I can tell by the writing that this _____ is mine.
11. Look at the _____ I made in art.
12. His _____ blew away because of the strong wind.

*Answers will vary.*

**6**

## Page 7

### Proper Nouns

**Proper nouns** name specific persons, places or things.

**Examples:**

**person** — Ms. Steiner, Judge Jones, Lt. Raydon
**place** — Crestview School, California, China
**thing** — Declaration of Independence, Encyclopedia Britannica

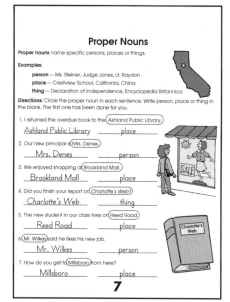

**Directions:** Circle the proper noun in each sentence. Write person, place or thing in the blank. The first one has been done for you.

1. I returned the overdue book to the (Ashland Public Library.)
   Ashland Public Library — place
2. Our new principal is (Mrs. Denes.)
   Mrs. Denes — person
3. We enjoyed shopping at (Brookland Mall.)
   Brookland Mall — place
4. Did you finish your report on (Charlotte's Web?)
   Charlotte's Web — thing
5. The new student in our class lives on (Reed Road.)
   Reed Road — place
6. (Mr. Wilkes) said he likes his new job.
   Mr. Wilkes — person
7. How do you get to (Millsboro) from here?
   Millsboro — place

**7**

## Page 8

### Proper Nouns: Capitalization

Proper nouns always begin with a capital letter.

**Examples:**

Monday
Texas
Karen
Mr. Logan
Hamburger Avenue
Rover

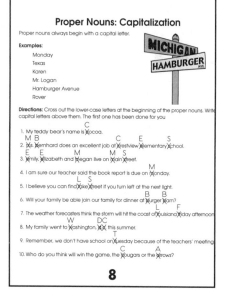

**Directions:** Cross out the lower-case letters at the beginning of the proper nouns. Write capital letters above them. The first one has been done for you.

1. My teddy bear's name is X̶cocoa. (C)
2. X̶s. X̶ernhard does an excellent job at X̶restview X̶lementary X̶chool. (M B / C E S)
3. X̶mily, X̶lizabeth and X̶egan live on X̶ain X̶treet. (E E M M S)
4. I am sure our teacher said the book report is due on X̶onday. (M)
5. I believe you can find X̶ake X̶treet if you turn left at the next light. (L S)
6. Will your family be able to join our family for dinner at X̶urger X̶arn? (B B)
7. The weather forecasters think the storm will hit the coast of X̶ouisiana X̶riday afternoon. (L F)
8. My family went to X̶ashington, X̶X̶ this summer. (W DC)
9. Remember, we don't have school on X̶uesday because of the teachers' meeting. (T)
10. Who do you think will win the game, the X̶ougars or the X̶rrows? (C A)

**8**

## Page 9

### Pronouns

A **pronoun** is a word that takes the place of a noun in a sentence.

**Examples:**

I, my, mine, me
we, our, ours, us
you, your, yours
he, his, him
she, her, hers
it, its
they, their, theirs, them

**Directions:** Underline the pronouns in each sentence.

1. Bring them to us as soon as you are finished.
2. She has been my best friend for many years.
3. They should be here soon.
4. We enjoyed our trip to the Mustard Museum.
5. Would you be able to help us with the project on Saturday?
6. Our homeroom teacher will not be here tomorrow.
7. My uncle said that he will be leaving soon for Australia.
8. Hurry! Could you please open the door for him?
9. She dropped her gloves when she got off the bus.
10. I can't figure out who the mystery writer is today.

**9**

## Page 10

### Nouns and Pronouns

To make a story or report more interesting, pronouns can be substituted for "overused" nouns.

**Example:**

Mother made the beds. Then Mother started the laundry.

The noun **Mother** is used in both sentences. The pronoun **she** could be used in place of **Mother** the second time to make the second sentence more interesting.

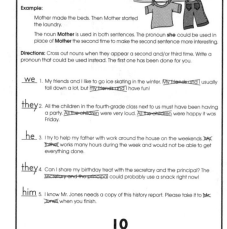

**Directions:** Cross out nouns when they appear a second and/or third time. Write a pronoun that could be used instead. The first one has been done for you.

we 1. My friends and I like to go ice skating in the winter. ~~My friends and I~~ usually fall down a lot, but ~~my friends and I~~ have fun!

they 2. All the children in the fourth-grade class next to us must have been having a party. ~~All the children~~ were very loud. ~~All the children~~ were happy it was Friday.

he 3. I try to help my father with work around the house on the weekends. ~~My father~~ works many hours during the week and would not be able to get everything done.

they 4. Can I share my birthday treat with the secretary and the principal? The ~~secretary and the principal~~ could probably use a snack right now!

him 5. I know Mr. Jones needs a copy of this history report. Please take it to ~~Mr. Jones~~ when you finish.

**10**

## Page 11

### Subjects and Predicates

The **subject** tells who or what the sentence is about. The **predicate** tells what the subject does, did, is doing or will do. A complete sentence must have a subject and a predicate.

**Examples:**

| Subject | Predicate |
|---|---|
| Sharon | writes to her grandmother every week. |
| The horse | ran around the track quickly. |
| My mom's car | is bright green. |
| Denise | will be here after lunch. |

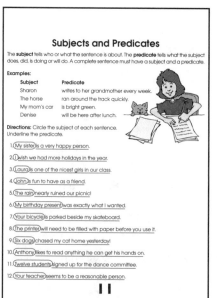

**Directions:** Circle the subject of each sentence. Underline the predicate.

1. (My sister) is a very happy person.
2. (I) wish we had more holidays in the year.
3. (Laura) is one of the nicest girls in our class.
4. (John) is fun to have as a friend.
5. (The rain) nearly ruined our picnic!
6. (My birthday present) was exactly what I wanted.
7. (Your bicycle) is parked beside my skateboard.
8. (The printer) will need to be filled with paper before you use it.
9. (Six dogs) chased my cat home yesterday!
10. (Anthony) likes to read anything he can get his hands on.
11. (Twelve students) signed up for the dance committee.
12. (Your teacher) seems to be a reasonable person.

**11**

## Subjects and Predicates

**Directions:** Write subjects to complete the following sentences.

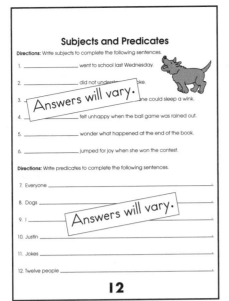

1. _____ went to school last Wednesday.
2. _____ did not underst~~___~~ ~~___~~ke.
3. _____ ~~___~~ one could sleep a wink.
4. _____ felt unhappy when the ball game was rained out.
5. _____ wonder what happened at the end of the book.
6. _____ jumped for joy when she won the contest.

*Answers will vary.*

**Directions:** Write predicates to complete the following sentences.

7. Everyone _____
8. Dogs _____
9. I _____

*Answers will vary.*

10. Justin _____
11. Jokes _____
12. Twelve people _____

**12**

## Subjects and Predicates

A **sentence** is a group of words that expresses a complete thought. It must have at least one subject and one verb.

**Examples:**

    **Sentence:** John felt tired and went to bed early.

    **Not a sentence:** Went to bed early.

**Directions:** Write **S** if the group of words is a complete sentence. Write **NS** if the group of words is not a sentence.

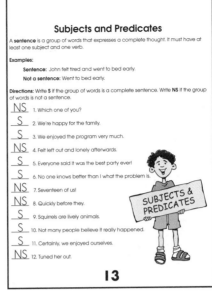

**NS** 1. Which one of you?
**S** 2. We're happy for the family.
**S** 3. We enjoyed the program very much.
**NS** 4. Felt left out and lonely afterwards.
**S** 5. Everyone said it was the best party ever!
**S** 6. No one knows better than I what the problem is.
**NS** 7. Seventeen of us!
**NS** 8. Quickly before they.
**S** 9. Squirrels are lively animals.
**S** 10. Not many people believe it really happened.
**S** 11. Certainly, we enjoyed ourselves.
**NS** 12. Tuned her out.

**SUBJECTS & PREDICATES**

**13**

## Compound Subjects

A **compound subject** is a subject with two parts joined by the word **and** or another conjunction. Compound subjects share the same predicate.

**Example:**

    Her shoes were covered with mud. Her ankles were covered with mud, too.

    **Compound subject:** Her shoes and ankles were covered with mud.
    The predicate in both sentences is **were covered with mud.**

**Directions:** Combine each pair of sentences into one sentence with a compound subject.

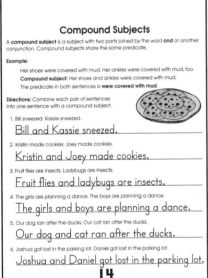

1. Bill sneezed. Kassie sneezed.
   Bill and Kassie sneezed.
2. Kristin made cookies. Joey made cookies.
   Kristin and Joey made cookies.
3. Fruit flies are insects. Ladybugs are insects.
   Fruit flies and ladybugs are insects.
4. The girls are planning a dance. The boys are planning a dance.
   The girls and boys are planning a dance.
5. Our dog ran after the ducks. Our cat ran after the ducks.
   Our dog and cat ran after the ducks.
6. Joshua got lost in the parking lot. Daniel got lost in the parking lot.
   Joshua and Daniel got lost in the parking lot.

**14**

## Compound Predicates

A **compound predicate** is a predicate with two parts joined by the word **and** or another conjunction. Compound predicates share the same subject.

**Example:** The baby grabbed the ball. The baby threw the ball.
    **Compound predicate:** The baby grabbed the ball and threw it.
    The subject in both sentences is **the baby.**

**Directions:** Combine each pair of sentences into one sentence to make a compound predicate.

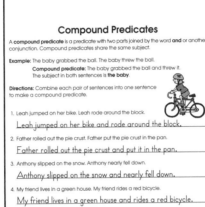

1. Leah jumped on her bike. Leah rode around the block.
   Leah jumped on her bike and rode around the block.
2. Father rolled out the pie crust. Father put the pie crust in the pan.
   Father rolled out the pie crust and put it in the pan.
3. Anthony slipped on the snow. Anthony nearly fell down.
   Anthony slipped on the snow and nearly fell down.
4. My friend lives in a green house. My friend rides a red bicycle.
   My friend lives in a green house and rides a red bicycle.
5. I opened the magazine. I began to read it quietly.
   I opened the magazine and began to read it quietly.
6. My father bought a new plaid shirt. My father wore his new red tie.
   My father bought a new plaid shirt and wore his new red tie.

**15**

## Intransitive Verbs

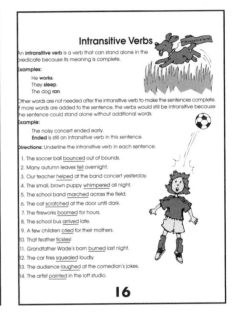

An **intransitive verb** is a verb that can stand alone in the predicate because its meaning is complete.

**Examples:**

    He **works.**
    They **sleep.**
    The dog **ran.**

Other words are not needed after the intransitive verb to make the sentences complete. If more words are added to the sentence, the verbs would still be intransitive because the sentence could stand alone without additional words.

**Example:**

    The noisy concert ended early.
    **Ended** is still an intransitive verb in this sentence.

**Directions:** Underline the intransitive verb in each sentence.

1. The soccer ball bounced out of bounds.
2. Many autumn leaves fell overnight.
3. Our teacher helped at the band concert yesterday.
4. The small, brown puppy whimpered all night.
5. The school band marched across the field.
6. The cat scratched at the door until dark.
7. The fireworks boomed for hours.
8. The school bus arrived late.
9. A few children cried for their mothers.
10. That feather tickles!
11. Grandfather Wade's barn burned last night.
12. The car tires squealed loudly.
13. The audience laughed at the comedian's jokes.
14. The artist painted in the loft studio.

**16**

## Transitive Verbs

A **transitive verb** needs a direct object to complete its meaning. A **direct object** is the word or words that come after a transitive verb to complete its meaning.

**Examples:**

    Tim **is** taking dance lessons.
    He **did** a dance.
    The dance **was** a gig.
    **Is, did** and **was** are transitive verbs. They must have one or more words after them to complete their meanings.

**Example:**

    The bird **found its nest.**
    The words **its nest** are needed after the transitive verb **found** to make the sentence complete.

**Directions:** Underline the transitive verb in each sentence.

1. The computer made a strange sound.
2. Last night's thunderstorm ruined our sand castles.
3. Aunt Jean raised tomatoes in her garden.
4. Brad accepted the award at the dinner last night.
5. Dad saw us outside his window.
6. The students in Home Economics baked delicious brownies.
7. We had a lot of homework.
8. He will replace the dead battery.
9. Everyone saw the special on television last night.
10. My dog chased the cat.
11. Morgan saw the kites flying high in the sky.
12. We enjoyed the museum trip.

**17**

## Intransitive and Transitive Verbs

**Directions:** Write a **T** in the blanks by the sentences that have a transitive verb. Write an **I** in the blanks by the sentences that have an intransitive verb.

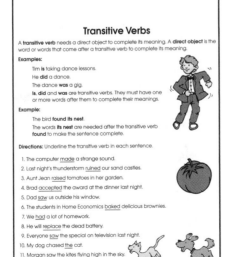

**T** 1. The story was a mystery.
**I** 2. The people cheered loudly.
**I** 3. The neighbor's dog barked yesterday.
**T** 4. We missed her birthday completely.
**I** 5. The lion roared.
**T** 6. Together, we sang many songs.
**T** 7. Elizabeth sharpened her pencil.
**T** 8. She visited New York City last summer.
**I** 9. The kitten cried for several hours.
**I** 10. Gina arrived late for school.
**I** 11. Did anyone cry when the mayor left?
**I** 12. The thunder boomed loudly.

**18**

*English and Grammar: Grade 4*

## Verbs: Present, Past and Future Tense

The **present tense** of a verb tells what is happening now.

**Examples:**
   I **am** happy.
   I **run** fast.

The **past tense** of a verb tells what has already happened.

**Examples:**
   I **was** happy.
   I **ran** fast.

The **future tense** of a verb refers to what is going to happen. The word **will** usually comes before the future tense of a verb.

**Examples:**
   I **will be** happy.
   I **will run** fast.

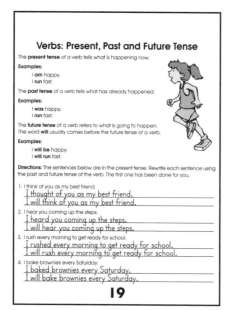

**Directions:** The sentences below are in the present tense. Rewrite each sentence using the past and future tense of the verb. The first one has been done for you.

1. I think of you as my best friend.
   I thought of you as my best friend.
   I will think of you as my best friend.
2. I hear you coming up the steps.
   I heard you coming up the steps.
   I will hear you coming up the steps.
3. I rush every morning to get ready for school.
   I rushed every morning to get ready for school.
   I will rush every morning to get ready for school.
4. I bake brownies every Saturday.
   I baked brownies every Saturday.
   I will bake brownies every Saturday.

**19**

---

## Verbs: Present, Past and Future Tense

**Directions:** Read the following sentences. Write **PRES** if the sentence is in present tense. Write **PAST** if the sentence is in past tense. Write **FUT** if the sentence is in future tense. The first one has been done for you.

FUT  1. I will be thrilled to accept the award.
FUT  2. Will you go with me to the dentist?
PAST 3. I thought he looked familiar!
PAST 4. They ate every single slice of pizza.
PRES 5. I run myself ragged sometimes.
PRES 6. Do you think this project is worthwhile?
PAST 7. No one has been able to repair the broken plate.
PRES 8. Thoughtful gifts are always appreciated.
PAST 9. I like the way he sang!
FUT  10. With a voice like that, he will go a long way.
PRES 11. It's my fondest hope that they visit soon.
PAST 12. I wanted that coat very much.
FUT  13. She'll be happy to take your place.
PRES 14. Everyone thinks the test will be a breeze.
PRES 15. Collecting stamps is her favorite hobby.

**20**

---

## Adding "ed" to Make Verbs Past Tense

To make many verbs past tense, add **ed**.

**Examples:**
  cook + ed = cooked  wish + ed = wished  play + ed = played

When a verb ends in a **silent e**, drop the **e** and add **ed**.

**Examples:**
  hope + ed = hoped  hate + ed = hated

When a verb ends in **y** after a consonant, change the **y** to **i** and add **ed**.

**Examples:**
  hurry + ed = hurried  marry + ed = married

When a verb ends in a single consonant after a single short vowel, double the final consonant before adding **ed**.

**Examples:**
  stop + ed = stopped  hop + ed = hopped

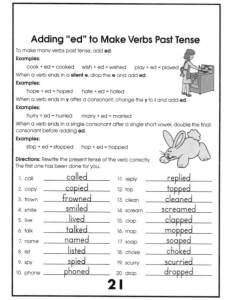

**Directions:** Rewrite the present tense of the verb correctly. The first one has been done for you.

| | | | | |
|---|---|---|---|---|
| 1. call | called | 11. reply | replied |
| 2. copy | copied | 12. top | topped |
| 3. frown | frowned | 13. clean | cleaned |
| 4. smile | smiled | 14. scream | screamed |
| 5. live | lived | 15. clap | clapped |
| 6. talk | talked | 16. mop | mopped |
| 7. name | named | 17. soap | soaped |
| 8. list | listed | 18. choke | choked |
| 9. spy | spied | 19. scurry | scurried |
| 10. phone | phoned | 20. drop | dropped |

**21**

---

## Verbs With "ed"

**Directions:** All the sentences below need a **verb + ed**. Write a word from the box to complete each sentence.

| talked | watched | served | wagged |
|---|---|---|---|
| picked | shared | typed | washed |
| | knocked | laughed | bothered |

1. She __talked__ on the phone for at least 1 hour.
2. He __washed__ the vegetables while I prepared the broth for the soup.
3. We never __laughed__ as hard as we did at that clown!
4. Each boy in the class __shared__ a story about what he had done over the summer.
5. Father __served__ the popcorn while Mother put the movie in the VCR.
6. I know that noise __bothered__ you last night.
7. The dog's tail __wagged__ so hard it __knocked__ over the picture on the table.
8. Do you know who __picked__ the flowers?
9. She carefully __typed__ her report for health class on the computer.
10. The whole class __watched__ as the rockets shot up into the sky.

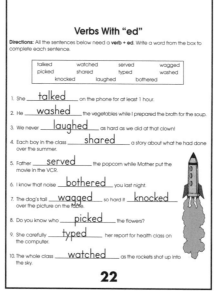

**22**

---

## Irregular Verbs: Past Tense

**Irregular verbs** change completely in the past tense. Unlike regular verbs, past-tense forms of irregular verbs are not formed by adding **ed**.

**Example:** The past tense of **go** is **went**.

Other verbs change some letters to form the past tense.
**Example:** The past tense of **break** is **broke**.

A **helping verb** helps to tell about the past. **Has**, **have**, and **had** are helping verbs used with action verbs to show the action occurred in the past. The past-tense form of the irregular verb sometimes changes when a helping verb is added.

| Present Tense Irregular Verb | Past Tense Irregular Verb | Past Tense Irregular Verb With Helper |
|---|---|---|
| go | went | have/has/had gone |
| see | saw | have/has/had seen |
| do | did | have/has/had done |
| bring | brought | have/has/had brought |
| sing | sang | have/has/had sung |
| drive | drove | have/has/had driven |
| swim | swam | have/has/had swum |
| sleep | slept | have/has/had slept |

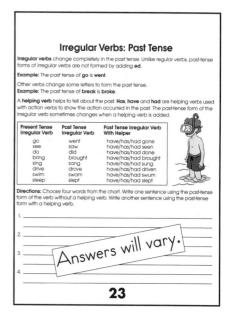

**Directions:** Choose four words from the chart. Write one sentence using the past-tense form of the verb without a helping verb. Write another sentence using the past-tense form with a helping verb.

1.
2.
3. Answers will vary.
4.

**23**

---

## The Irregular Verb "Be"

**Be** is an irregular verb. The present-tense forms of be are **be**, **am**, **is** and **are**. The past-tense forms of **be** are **was** and **were**.

**Directions:** Write the correct form of **be** in the blanks. The first one has been done for you.

1. I __am__ so happy for you!
2. Jared __was__ unfriendly yesterday.
3. English can __be__ a lot of fun to learn.
4. They __are__ among the nicest people I know.
5. They __were__ late yesterday.
6. She promises she __is__ going to arrive on time.
7. I __am__ nervous right now about the test.
8. If you __are__ satisfied now, so am I.
9. He __was__ as nice to me last week as I had hoped.
10. He can __be__ very gracious.
11. Would you __be__ offended if I moved your desk?
12. He __was__ watching at the window for me yesterday.

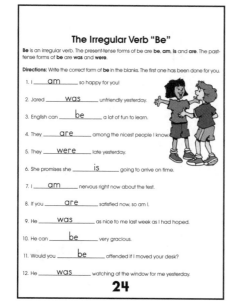

**24**

---

## Verbs: "Was" and "Were"

| Singular | Plural |
|---|---|
| I was | we were |
| you were | you were |
| he, she, it was | they were |

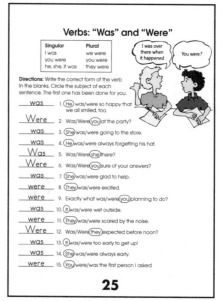

**Directions:** Write the correct form of the verb in the blanks. Circle the subject of each sentence. The first one has been done for you.

was  1. (He) was/were so happy that we all smiled, too.
Were 2. Was/Were (you) at the party?
was  3. (She) was/were going to the store.
was  4. (He) was/were always forgetting his hat.
Was  5. Was/Were (she) there?
Were 6. Was/Were (you) sure of your answers?
was  7. (She) was/were glad to help.
were 8. (They) was/were excited.
were 9. Exactly what was/were (you) planning to do?
was  10. (It) was/were wet outside.
were 11. (They) was/were scared by the noise.
Were 12. Was/Were (they) expected before noon?
was  13. (It) was/were too early to get up!
was  14. (She) was/were always early.
were 15. (You) were/was the first person I asked.

**25**

---

## Verbs: "Went" and "Gone"

The word **went** is used without a helping verb.

**Examples:**
Correct: Susan **went** to the store.
Incorrect: Susan **has went** to the store.

**Gone** is used with a helping verb.

**Examples:**
Correct: Susan **has gone** to the store.
Incorrect: Susan **gone** to the store.

**Directions:** Write **C** in the blank if the verb is used correctly. Draw an **X** in the blank if the verb is not used correctly.

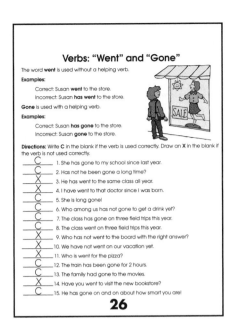

__C__ 1. She has gone to my school since last year.
__C__ 2. Has not he been a long time?
__X__ 3. He has went to the same class all year.
__X__ 4. I have went to that doctor since I was born.
__C__ 5. She is long gone!
__C__ 6. Who among us has not gone to get a drink yet?
__C__ 7. The class has gone on three field trips this year.
__C__ 8. The class went on three field trips this year.
__X__ 9. Who has not went to the board with the right answer?
__X__ 10. We have not went on our vacation yet.
__X__ 11. Who is went for the pizza?
__C__ 12. The train has been gone for 2 hours.
__C__ 13. The family had gone to the movies.
__X__ 14. Have you went to visit the new bookstore?
__C__ 15. He has gone on and on about how smart you are!

**26**

## Direct Objects

A **direct object** is the word or words that come after a transitive verb to complete its meaning. The direct object answers the question **whom** or **what**.

**Examples:**
Aaron wrote a **letter**.
**Letter** is the direct object. It tells what Aaron wrote.
We heard **Tom**.
**Tom** is the direct object. It tells whom we heard.

**Directions:** Identify the direct object in each sentence. Write it in the blank.

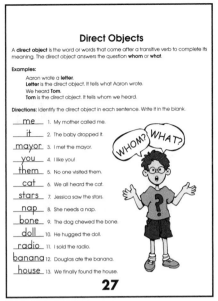

__me__ 1. My mother called me.
__it__ 2. The baby dropped it.
__mayor__ 3. I met the mayor.
__you__ 4. I like you!
__them__ 5. No one visited them.
__cat__ 6. We all heard the cat.
__stars__ 7. Jessica saw the stars.
__nap__ 8. She needs a nap.
__bone__ 9. The dog chewed the bone.
__doll__ 10. He hugged the doll.
__radio__ 11. I sold the radio.
__banana__ 12. Douglas ate the banana.
__house__ 13. We finally found the house.

**27**

## Indirect Objects

An **indirect object** is the word or words that come between the verb and the direct object. Indirect objects tells **to whom** or **what** or **for whom** or **what** something is done.

**Examples:**
He read **me** a funny story.
**Me** is the indirect object. It tells to whom something (reading a story) was done.
She told her **mother** the truth.
**Mother** is the indirect object. It tells to whom something (telling the truth) was done.

**Directions:** Identify the indirect object in each sentence. Write it in the blank.

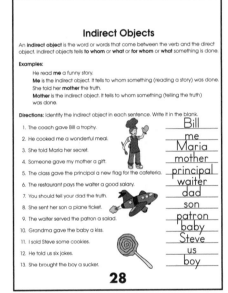

1. The coach gave Bill a trophy. — Bill
2. He cooked me a wonderful meal. — me
3. She told Maria her secret. — Maria
4. Someone gave my mother a gift. — mother
5. The class gave the principal a new flag for the cafeteria. — principal
6. The restaurant pays the waiter a good salary. — waiter
7. You should tell your dad the truth. — dad
8. She sent her son a plane ticket. — son
9. The waiter served the patron a salad. — patron
10. Grandma gave the baby a kiss. — baby
11. I sold Steve some cookies. — Steve
12. He told us six jokes. — us
13. She brought the boy a sucker. — boy

**28**

## Direct and Indirect Objects

**Example:** Sharon told Jennifer a funny (story).

Jennifer is the indirect object. It tells **to whom** Sharon told the story. Story is the direct object. It tells **what** Sharon told.

**Directions:** Circle the direct object in each sentence. Underline the indirect object.

1. The teacher gave the class a (test).
2. Josh brought Elizabeth the (book).
3. Someone left the cat a (present).
4. The poet read David all his (poems).
5. My big brother handed me the (ticket).
6. Luke told everyone the (secret).
7. Jason handed his dad the (newspaper).
8. Mother bought Jack a (suitcase).
9. They cooked us an excellent (dinner).
10. I loaned Jonathan my (bike).
11. She threw him a curve (ball).
12. You tell Dad the (truth).

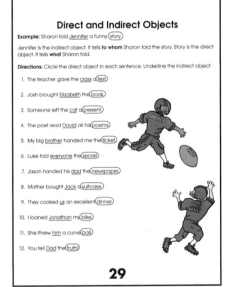

**29**

## Adverbs

**Adverbs** are words that tell when, where or how.

**Adverbs of time** tell when.
**Example:**
The train left yesterday.
**Yesterday** is an adverb of time. It tells when the train left.

**Adverbs of place** tell where.
**Example:**
The girl walked away.
**Away** is an adverb of place. It tells where the girl walked.

**Adverbs of manner** tell how.
**Example:**
The boy walked quickly.
**Quickly** is an adverb of manner. It tells how the boy walked.

**Directions:** Write the adverb for each sentence in the first blank. In the second blank, write where it is an adverb of time, place or manner. The first one has been done for you.

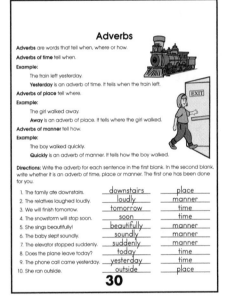

| | | |
|---|---|---|
| 1. The family ate downstairs. | downstairs | place |
| 2. The relatives laughed loudly. | loudly | manner |
| 3. We will finish tomorrow. | tomorrow | time |
| 4. The snowstorm will stop soon. | soon | time |
| 5. She sings beautifully! | beautifully | manner |
| 6. The baby slept soundly. | soundly | manner |
| 7. The elevator stopped suddenly. | suddenly | manner |
| 8. Does the plane leave today? | today | time |
| 9. The phone call came yesterday. | yesterday | time |
| 10. She ran outside. | outside | place |

**30**

## Adverbs of Time

**Directions:** Choose a word or group of words from the box to complete each sentence. Make sure the adverb you choose makes sense with the rest of the sentence.

| | |
|---|---|
| in 2 weeks | last winter |
| next week | at the end of the day |
| soon | right now |
| 2 days ago | tonight |

**Sample answers:**

1. We had a surprise birthday party for him **2 days ago**
2. Our science projects are due **in 2 weeks**
3. My best friend will be moving **next week**
4. Justin and Ronnie need our help **right now** !
5. We will find out who the winners are **at the end of the day**
6. Can you take me to ball practice **tonight** ?
7. She said we will be getting a letter **soon**
8. Diane made the quilt **last winter**

**31**

## Adverbs of Place

**Directions:** Choose one word from the box to complete each sentence. Make sure the adverb you choose makes sense with the rest of the sentence.

| | | | |
|---|---|---|---|
| inside | upstairs | below | everywhere |
| home | somewhere | outside | there |

**Sample answers:**

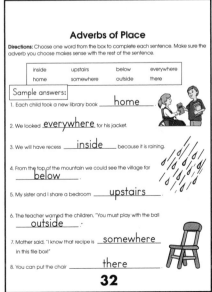

1. Each child took a new library book **home**
2. We looked **everywhere** for his jacket.
3. We will have recess **inside** because it is raining.
4. From the top of the mountain we could see the village far **below**
5. My sister and I share a bedroom **upstairs**
6. The teacher warned the children, "You must play with the ball **outside**
7. Mother said, "I know that recipe is **somewhere** in this file box!"
8. You can put the chair **there**

**32**

*English and Grammar: Grade 4*

## Adverbs of Manner

**Directions:** Choose a word from the box to complete each sentence. Make sure the adverb you choose makes sense with the rest of the sentence. One word will be used twice.

| quickly | carefully | loudly | easily | carelessly | slowly |

Sample answers:

1. The scouts crossed the old bridge **carefully**.

2. We watched the turtle move **slowly** across the yard.

3. Everyone completed the math test **quickly**.

4. The quarterback scampered **easily** down the sideline.

5. The mother **carefully** cleaned the child's sore knee.

6. The fire was caused by someone **carelessly** tossing a match.

7. The alarm rang **loudly** while we were eating.

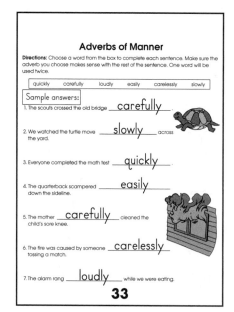

**33**

---

## Adjectives That Add "er"

The suffix **er** is often added to adjectives to compare two things.

**Example:**

My feet are **large**.

Your feet are **larger** than my feet.

When a one-syllable adjective ends in a single consonant and the vowel is short, double the final consonant before adding **er**. When a word ends in two or more consonants, add **er**.

**Examples:**

big — bigger (single consonant)

bold — bolder (two consonants)

When an adjective ends in **y**, change the **y** to **i** before adding **er**.

**Examples:**

easy — easier

greasy — greasier

breezy — breezier

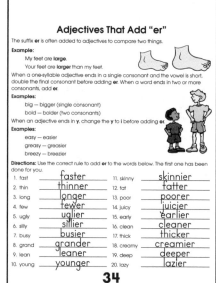

**Directions:** Use the correct rule to add **er** to the words below. The first one has been done for you.

1. fast **faster**
2. thin **thinner**
3. long **longer**
4. few **fewer**
5. ugly **uglier**
6. silly **sillier**
7. busy **busier**
8. grand **grander**
9. lean **leaner**
10. young **younger**
11. skinny **skinnier**
12. fat **fatter**
13. poor **poorer**
14. juicy **juicier**
15. early **earlier**
16. clean **cleaner**
17. thick **thicker**
18. creamy **creamier**
19. deep **deeper**
20. lazy **lazier**

**34**

---

## Adjectives That Add "est"

The suffix **est** is often added to adjectives to compare more than two things.

**Example:**

My glass is **full**.

Your glass is **fuller**.

His glass is **fullest**.

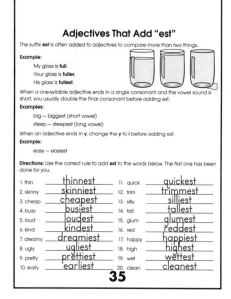

When a one-syllable adjective ends in a single consonant and the vowel sound is short, you usually double the final consonant before adding est.

**Examples:**

big — biggest (short vowel)

steep — steepest (long vowel)

When an adjective ends in **y**, change the **y** to **i** before adding **est**.

**Example:**

easy — easiest

**Directions:** Use the correct rule to add **est** to the words below. The first one has been done for you.

1. thin **thinnest**
2. skinny **skinniest**
3. cheap **cheapest**
4. busy **busiest**
5. loud **loudest**
6. kind **kindest**
7. dreamy **dreamiest**
8. ugly **ugliest**
9. pretty **prettiest**
10. early **earliest**
11. quick **quickest**
12. trim **trimmest**
13. silly **silliest**
14. tall **tallest**
15. glum **glumest**
16. red **reddest**
17. happy **happiest**
18. high **highest**
19. wet **wettest**
20. clean **cleanest**

**35**

---

## Adding "er" and "est" to Adjectives

**Directions:** Circle the correct adjective for each sentence. The first one has been done for you.

1. Of all the students in the gym, her voice was (louder, **loudest**).

2. "I can tell you are (**busier**, busiest) than I am," he said to the librarian.

3. If you and Carl stand back to back, I can see which one is (**taller**, tallest).

4. She is the (kinder, **kindest**) teacher in the whole building.

5. Wow! That is the (bigger, **biggest**) pumpkin I have ever seen!

6. I believe your flashlight is (**brighter**, brightest) than mine.

7. "This is the (cleaner, **cleanest**) your room has been in a long time," Mother said.

8. The leaves on that plant are (**prettier**, prettiest) than the ones on the window sill.

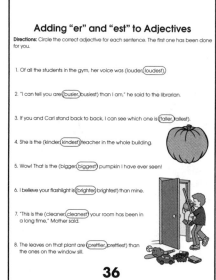

**36**

---

## Adjectives Preceded by "More"

Most adjectives of two or more syllables are preceded by the word **more** as a way to show comparison between two things.

**Examples:**

Correct: intelligent, more intelligent

Incorrect: intelligenter

Correct: famous, more famous

Incorrect: famouser

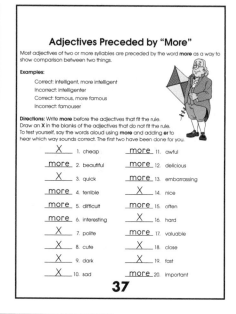

**Directions:** Write **more** before the adjectives that fit the rule. Draw an **X** in the blanks of the adjectives that do not fit the rule. To test yourself, say the words aloud using **more** and adding **er** to hear which way sounds correct. The first two have been done for you.

1. **X** cheap
2. **more** beautiful
3. **X** quick
4. **more** terrible
5. **more** difficult
6. **more** interesting
7. **X** polite
8. **X** cute
9. **X** dark
10. **X** sad
11. **more** awful
12. **more** delicious
13. **more** embarrassing
14. **X** nice
15. **more** often
16. **X** hard
17. **more** valuable
18. **X** close
19. **X** fast
20. **more** important

**37**

---

## Adjectives Using "er" or "More"

**Directions:** Add the word or words needed in each sentence. The first one has been done for you.

1. I thought the book was **more interesting** than the movie. (interesting)

2. Do you want to carry this box? It is **lighter** than the one you have now. (light)

3. I noticed you are moving **slower** this morning. Does your ankle still bother you? (slow)

4. Thomas Edison is probably **more famous** for his invention of the electric light bulb than the phonograph. (famous)

5. She stuck out her lower lip and whined, "Your ice-cream cone is **bigger** than mine!" (big)

6. Mom said my room was **cleaner** than it has been in a long time. (clean)

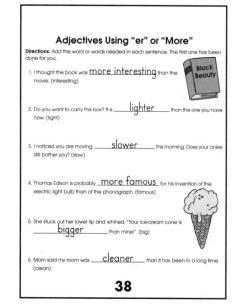

**38**

---

## Adjectives Preceded by "Most"

Most adjectives of two or more syllables are preceded by the word **most** as a way to show comparison between more than two things.

**Examples:**

| Correct: | intelligent, most intelligent |
| Incorrect: | intelligentest |
| Correct: | famous, most famous |
| Incorrect: | famousest |

**Directions:** Read the following groups of sentences. In the last sentence for each group, write the adjective preceded by **most**. The first one has been done for you.

1. My uncle is intelligent.
My aunt is more intelligent.
My cousin is the **most intelligent**.

2. I am thankful.
My brother is more thankful.
My parents are the **most thankful**.

3. Your sister is polite.
Your brother is more polite.
You are the **most polite**.

4. The blouse was expensive.
The sweater was more expensive.
The coat was the **most expensive**.

5. The class was fortunate.
The teacher was more fortunate.
The principal was the **most fortunate**.

6. The cookies were delicious.
The cake was even more delicious.
The brownies were the **most delicious**.

7. That painting is elaborate.
The sculpture is more elaborate.
The finger painting is the **most elaborate**.

**39**

---

## Adjectives Using "est" or "Most"

**Directions:** Add the word or words needed to complete each sentence. The first one has been done for you.

1. The star over there is the ___brightest___ of all. (bright)

2. "I believe this is the ___most delightful___ time I have ever had," said Mackenzie. (delightful)

3. That game was the ___most exciting___ one of the whole year! (exciting)

4. I think this tree has the ___greenest___ leaves. (green)

5. We will need the ___sharpest___ knife you have to cut the face for the jack-o-lantern. (sharp)

6. Everyone agreed that your chocolate chip cookies were the ___most delicious___ of all. (delicious)

**40**

---

## Adjectives and Adverbs

**Directions:** Write **ADJ** on the line if the bold word is an adjective. Write **ADV** if the bold word is an adverb. The first one has been done for you.

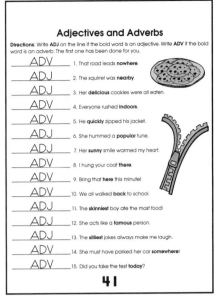

___ADV___ 1. That road leads **nowhere**.

___ADJ___ 2. The squirrel was **nearby**.

___ADJ___ 3. Her **delicious** cookies were all eaten.

___ADV___ 4. Everyone rushed **indoors**.

___ADV___ 5. He **quickly** zipped his jacket.

___ADJ___ 6. She hummed a **popular** tune.

___ADJ___ 7. Her **sunny** smile warmed my heart.

___ADV___ 8. I hung your coat **there**.

___ADV___ 9. Bring that **here** this minute!

___ADV___ 10. We all walked **back** to school.

___ADJ___ 11. The **skinniest** boy ate the most food!

___ADJ___ 12. She acts like a **famous** person.

___ADJ___ 13. The **silliest** jokes always make me laugh.

___ADV___ 14. She must have parked her car **somewhere**!

___ADV___ 15. Did you take the test **today**?

**41**

---

## "Good" and "Well"

Use the word **good** to describe a noun. Good is an adjective.

**Example:** She is a **good** teacher.

Use the word **well** to tell or ask how something is done or to describe someone's health. Well is an adverb. It describes a verb.

**Example:** She is not feeling **well**.

**Directions:** Write **good** or **well** in the blanks to complete the sentences correctly. The first one has been done for you.

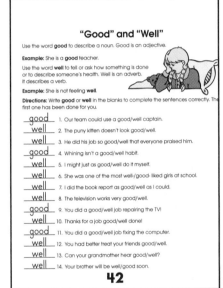

___good___ 1. Our team could use a good/well captain.

___well___ 2. The puny kitten doesn't look good/well.

___well___ 3. He did his job so good/well that everyone praised him.

___good___ 4. Whining isn't a good/well habit.

___well___ 5. I might just as good/well do it myself.

___well___ 6. She was one of the most well-/good- liked girls at school.

___well___ 7. I did the book report as good/well as I could.

___well___ 8. The television works very good/well.

___good___ 9. You did a good/well job repairing the TV!

___well___ 10. Thanks for a job good/well done!

___good___ 11. You did a good/well job fixing the computer.

___well___ 12. You had better treat your friends good/well.

___well___ 13. Can your grandmother hear good/well?

___well___ 14. Your brother will be good/well soon.

**42**

---

## "Your" and "You're"

The word **your** shows possession.

**Examples:**

Is that **your** book?

I visited **your** class.

The word **you're** is a contraction for **you are**. A contraction is two words joined together as one. An apostrophe shows where letters have been left out.

**Examples:**

**You're** doing well on that painting.

If **you're** going to pass the test, you should study.

**Directions:** Write **your** or **you're** on the blanks to complete the sentences correctly. The first one has been done for you.

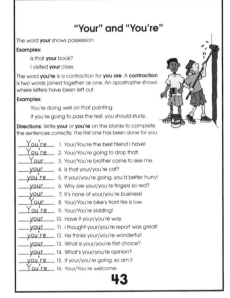

___You're___ 1. Your/You're the best friend I have!

___You're___ 2. Your/You're going to drop that!

___Your___ 3. Your/You're brother came to see me.

___your___ 4. Is that your/you're cat?

___you're___ 5. If your/you're going, you'd better hurry!

___your___ 6. Why are your/you're fingers so red?

___your___ 7. It's none of your/you're business!

___Your___ 8. Your/You're bike's front tire is low.

___You're___ 9. Your/You're kidding!

___your___ 10. Have it your/you're way.

___your___ 11. I thought your/you're report was great!

___you're___ 12. He thinks your/you're wonderful!

___your___ 13. What is your/you're first choice?

___your___ 14. What's your/you're opinion?

___you're___ 15. If your/you're going, so am I!

___You're___ 16. Your/You're welcome.

**43**

---

## "Good" and "Well"; "Your" and "You're"

**Directions:** Choose the correct word for each sentence: **good, well, your** or **you're**.

1. Are you sure you can see ___well___ enough to read with the lighting you have?

2. ___You're___ going to need a paint smock when you go to art class tomorrow afternoon.

3. I can see ___you're___ having some trouble. Can I help with that?

4. The music department needs to buy a speaker system that has ___good___ quality sound.

5. The principal asked, "Where is ___your___ hall pass?"

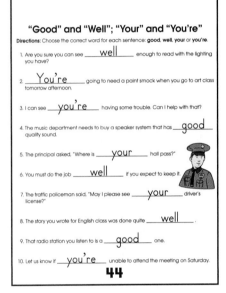

6. You must do the job ___well___ if you expect to keep it.

7. The traffic policeman said, "May I please see ___your___ driver's license?"

8. The story you wrote for English class was done quite ___well___ .

9. That radio station you listen to is a ___good___ one.

10. Let us know if ___you're___ unable to attend the meeting on Saturday.

**44**

---

## "Its" and "It's"

The word **its** shows ownership.

**Examples:**

**Its** leaves have all turned green.

**Its** paw was injured.

The word **it's** is a contraction for **it is**.

**Examples:**

**It's** better to be early than late.

**It's** not fair!

**Directions:** Write **its** or **it's** to complete the sentences correctly. The first one has been done for you.

___It's___ 1. Its/It's never too late for ice cream!

___Its___ 2. Its/It's eyes are already open.

___It's___ 3. Its/It's your turn to wash the dishes!

___Its___ 4. Its/It's cage was left open.

___Its___ 5. Its/It's engine was beyond repair.

___Its___ 6. Its/It's teeth were long and pointed.

___its___ 7. Did you see its/it's hind legs?

___it's___ 8. Why do you think its/it's mine?

___it's___ 9. Do you think its/it's the right color?

___its___ 10. Don't pet its/it's fur too hard!

___It's___ 11. Its/It's from my Uncle Harry.

___it's___ 12. Can you tell its/it's a surprise?

___its___ 13. Is its/it's stall always this clean?

___It's___ 14. Its/It's not time to eat yet.

___it's___ 15. She says its/it's working now.

**45**

---

## "Can" and "May"

The word **can** means am able to or to be able to.

**Examples:**

I **can** do that for you.

**Can** you do that for me?

The word **may** means be allowed to or permitted to. May is used to ask or give permission. **May** can also mean **might** or **perhaps**.

**Examples:**

**May** I be excused?

You **may** sit here.

**Directions:** Write **can** or **may** on the blanks to complete the sentences correctly. The first one has been done for you.

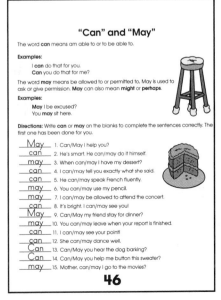

___May___ 1. Can/May I help you?

___can___ 2. He's smart. He can/may do it himself.

___may___ 3. When can/may I have my dessert?

___can___ 4. I can/may tell you exactly what she said.

___can___ 5. He can/may speak French fluently.

___may___ 6. You can/may use my pencil.

___may___ 7. I can/may be allowed to attend the concert.

___can___ 8. It's bright. I can/may see you!

___May___ 9. Can/May my friend stay for dinner?

___may___ 10. You can/may leave when your report is finished.

___can___ 11. I can/may see your point!

___can___ 12. She can/may dance well.

___Can___ 13. Can/May you hear the dog barking?

___Can___ 14. Can/May you help me button this sweater?

___may___ 15. Mother, can/may I go to the movies?

**46**

---

*English and Grammar: Grade 4*

## "Sit" and "Set"

The word **sit** means to rest.

**Examples:**

Please **sit** here!

Will you **sit** by me?

The word **set** means to put or place something.

**Examples:**

**Set** your purse there.

**Set** the dishes on the table.

**Directions:** Write **sit** or **set** to complete the sentences correctly. The first one has been done for you.

| | |
|---|---|
| sit | 1. Would you please sit/set down here? |
| set | 2. You can sit/set the groceries there. |
| set | 3. She sit/set her suitcase in the closet. |
| set | 4. He sit/set his watch for half past three. |
| sit | 5. She's a person who can't sit/set still. |
| set | 6. Sit/set the baby on the couch beside me. |
| set | 7. Where did you sit/set your new shoes? |
| sit | 8. They decided to sit/set together during the movie. |
| set | 9. Let me sit/set you straight on that! |
| sit | 10. Instead of swimming, he decided to sit/set in the water. |
| set | 11. He sit/set the greasy pan in the sink. |
| set | 12. She sit/set the file folder on her desk. |
| sit | 13. Don't ever sit/set on the refrigerator! |
| set | 14. She sit/set the candles on the cake. |
| set | 15. Get ready! Get sit/set! Go! |

**47**

## "They're," "Their," "There"

The word **they're** is a contraction for **they are**.

**Examples:**

**They're** our very best friends!

Ask them if **they're** coming over tomorrow.

The word **their** shows ownership.

**Examples:**

**Their** dog is friendly.

It's **their** bicycle.

The word **there** shows place or direction.

**Examples:**

Look over **there**.

**There** it is.

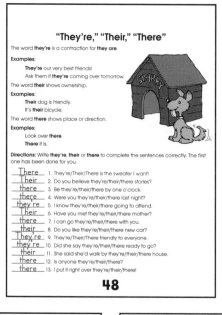

**Directions:** Write **they're**, **their** or **there** to complete the sentences correctly. The first one has been done for you.

| | |
|---|---|
| There | 1. They're/Their/There is the sweater I want! |
| Their | 2. Do you believe they're/their/there stories? |
| there | 3. Be they're/their/there by one o'clock. |
| there | 4. Were you they're/their/there last night? |
| they're | 5. I know they're/their/there going to attend. |
| Their | 6. Have you met they're/their/there mother? |
| there | 7. I can go they're/their/there with you. |
| their | 8. Do you like they're/their/there new car? |
| They're | 9. They're/Their/There friendly to everyone. |
| they're | 10. Did she say they're/their/there ready to go? |
| their | 11. She said she'd walk by they're/their/there house. |
| there | 12. Is anyone they're/their/there? |
| there | 13. I put it right over they're/their/there! |

**48**

## "This" and "These"

The word **this** is an adjective that refers to things that are near. **This** always describes a singular noun. Singular means one.

**Example:**

I'll buy **this** coat.

(Coat is singular.)

The word **these** is also an adjective that refers to things that are near. **These** always describes a plural noun. A plural refers to more than one thing.

**Example:**

I will buy **these** flowers.

(Flowers is a plural noun.)

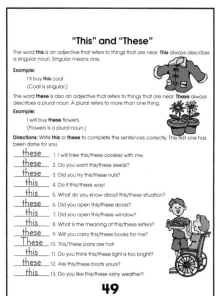

**Directions:** Write **this** or **these** to complete the sentences correctly. The first one has been done for you.

| | |
|---|---|
| these | 1. I will take this/these cookies with me. |
| these | 2. Do you want this/these seeds? |
| these | 3. Did you try this/these nuts? |
| this | 4. Do it this/these way! |
| this | 5. What do you know about this/these situation? |
| these | 6. Did you open this/these doors? |
| this | 7. Did you open this/these window? |
| this | 8. What is the meaning of this/these letters? |
| these | 9. Will you carry this/these books for me? |
| These | 10. This/These pans are hot! |
| this | 11. Do you think this/these light is too bright? |
| these | 12. Are this/these boots yours? |
| this | 13. Do you like this/these rainy weather? |

**49**

## Making Sense of Sentences

A **statement** is a sentence that tells something. It ends with a period (.).

**Example:** Columbus is the capital of Ohio.

A **question** is a sentence that asks something. It ends with a question mark (?).

**Example:** Do you like waffles?

An **exclamation** is a sentence that shows strong feeling. It ends with an exclamation mark (!).

**Example:** You're the best friend in the world!

A **command** is a sentence that orders someone to do something. It ends with a period or exclamation mark.

**Example:** Shut the door. Watch out for that trunk!

A **request** is a sentence that asks someone to do something. It ends with a period or question mark.

**Example:** Please shut the door.

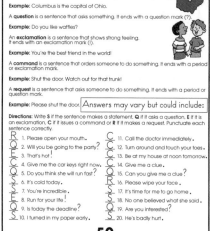

Answers may vary but could include:

**Directions:** Write **S** if the sentence makes a statement, **Q** if it asks a question, **E** if it is an exclamation, **C** if it issues a command or **R** if it makes a request. Punctuate each sentence correctly.

| | | | |
|---|---|---|---|
| R | 1. Please open your mouth. | C | 11. Call the doctor immediately. |
| Q | 2. Will you be going to the party? | C | 12. Turn around and touch your toes. |
| E | 3. That's hot! | C | 13. Be at my house at noon tomorrow. |
| C | 4. Give me the car keys right now. | C | 14. Give me a clue. |
| Q | 5. Do you think she will run fast? | Q | 15. Can you give me a clue? |
| S | 6. It's cold today. | R | 16. Please wipe your face. |
| E | 7. You're incredible. | S | 17. It's time for me to go home. |
| E | 8. Run for your life! | S | 18. No one believed what she said. |
| Q | 9. Is today the deadline? | Q | 19. Are you interested? |
| S | 10. I turned in my paper early. | S | 20. He's badly hurt. |

**50**

## Writing Question Sentences

**Directions:** Rewrite each sentence to make it a question. The first one has been done for you. In some cases, the form of the verb must be changed.

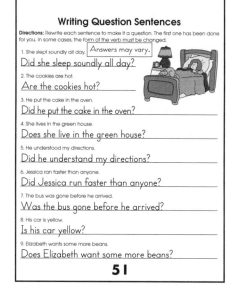

1. She slept soundly all day.   Answers may vary.

Did she sleep soundly all day?

2. The cookies are hot.

Are the cookies hot?

3. He put the cake in the oven.

Did he put the cake in the oven?

4. She lives in the green house.

Does she live in the green house?

5. He understood my directions.

Did he understand my directions?

6. Jessica ran faster than anyone.

Did Jessica run faster than anyone?

7. The bus was gone before he arrived.

Was the bus gone before he arrived?

8. His car is yellow.

Is his car yellow?

9. Elizabeth wants some more beans.

Does Elizabeth want some more beans?

**51**

## Conjunctions

Words that join sentences or combine ideas like **and**, **but**, **or**, **because**, **when**, **after** and **so** are called **conjunctions**.

**Examples:**

I played the drums, **and** Sue played the clarinet.

She likes bananas, **but** I do not.

We could play music **or** just enjoy the silence.

I needed the book **because** I had to write a book report.

He gave me the book **when** I asked for it.

I asked her to eat lunch **after** she finished the test.

You wanted my bike **so** you could ride it.

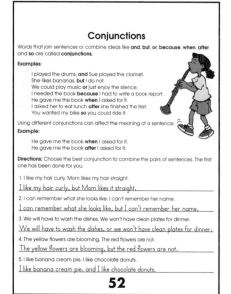

Using different conjunctions can affect the meaning of a sentence.

**Example:**

He gave me the book **when** I asked for it.

He gave me the book **after** I asked for it.

**Directions:** Choose the best conjunction to combine the pairs of sentences. The first one has been done for you.

1. I like my hair curly. Mom likes my hair straight.

I like my hair curly, but Mom likes it straight.

2. I can remember what she looks like. I can't remember her name.

I can remember what she looks like, but I can't remember her name.

3. We will have to wash the dishes. We won't have clean plates for dinner.

We will have to wash the dishes, or we won't have clean plates for dinner.

4. The yellow flowers are blooming. The red flowers are not.

The yellow flowers are blooming, but the red flowers are not.

5. I like banana cream pie. I like chocolate donuts.

I like banana cream pie, and I like chocolate donuts.

**52**

## "And," "But," "Or"

**Directions:** Write **and**, **but** or **or** to complete the sentences.

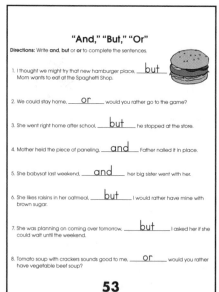

1. I thought we might try that new hamburger place, __but__ Mom wants to eat at the Spaghetti Shop.

2. We could stay home, __or__ would you rather go to the game?

3. She went right home after school, __but__ he stopped at the store.

4. Mother held the piece of paneling, __and__ Father nailed it in place.

5. She babysat last weekend, __and__ her big sister went with her.

6. She likes raisins in her oatmeal, __but__ I would rather have mine with brown sugar.

7. She was planning on coming over tomorrow, __but__ I asked her if she could wait until the weekend.

8. Tomato soup with crackers sounds good to me. __or__ would you rather have vegetable beef soup?

**53**

## "Because" and "So"

**Directions:** Write **because** or **so** to complete the sentences.

1. She cleaned the paint brushes ___so___ they would be ready in the morning.

2. Father called home complaining of a sore throat ___so___ Mom stopped by the pharmacy.

3. His bus will be running late ___because___ it has a flat tire.

4. We all worked together ___so___ we could get the job done sooner.

5. We took a variety of sandwiches on the picnic ___because___ we knew not everyone liked cheese and olives with mayonnaise.

6. All the school children were sent home ___because___ the electricity went off at school.

7. My brother wants us to meet his girlfriend ___so___ she will be coming to dinner with us on Friday.

8. He forgot to take his umbrella along this morning ___so___ now his clothes are very wet.

**54**

---

## "When" and "After"

**Directions:** Write **when** or **after** to complete the sentences.

Answers may vary.

1. I knew we were in trouble ___when___ I heard the thunder in the distance.

2. We carried the baskets of cherries to the car ___after___ we were finished picking them.

3. Mother took off her apron ___after___ I reminded her that our dinner guests would be here any minute.

4. I wondered if we would have school tomorrow ___after___ I noticed the snow begin to fall.

5. The boys and girls all clapped ___when___ the magician pulled the colored scarves out of his sleeve.

6. I was startled ___when___ the phone rang so late last night.

7. You will need to get the film developed ___after___ you have taken all the pictures.

8. The children began to run ___when___ the snake started to move!

**55**

---

## Conjunctions

**Directions:** Choose the best conjunction from the box to combine the pairs of sentences. Then rewrite the sentences.

| and | but | or | because | when | after | so |
|---|---|---|---|---|---|---|

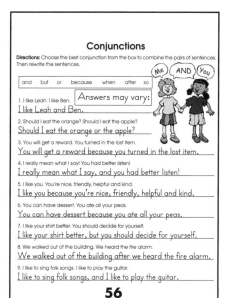

Answers may vary:

1. I like Leah. I like Ben.
I like Leah and Ben.

2. Should I eat the orange? Should I eat the apple?
Should I eat the orange or the apple?

3. You will get a reward. You turned in the lost item.
You will get a reward because you turned in the lost item.

4. I really mean what I say! You had better listen!
I really mean what I say, and you had better listen!

5. I like you. You're nice, friendly, helpful and kind.
I like you because you're nice, friendly, helpful and kind.

6. You can have dessert. You ate all your peas.
You can have dessert because you ate all your peas.

7. I like your shirt better. You should decide for yourself.
I like your shirt better, but you should decide for yourself.

8. We walked out of the building. We heard the fire alarm.
We walked out of the building after we heard the fire alarm.

9. I like to sing folk songs. I like to play the guitar.
I like to sing folk songs, and I like to play the guitar.

**56**

---

## Run-On Sentences

A **run-on sentence** occurs when two or more sentences are joined together without punctuation.

**Examples:**

**Run-on sentence:** I lost my way once did you?
**Two sentences with correct punctuation:** I lost my way once. Did you?
**Run-on sentence:** I found the recipe it was not hard to follow.
**Two sentences with correct punctuation:** I found the recipe. It was not hard to follow.

**Directions:** Rewrite the run-on sentences correctly with periods, exclamation points and question marks. The first one has been done for you.

1. Did you take my umbrella I can't find it anywhere!
Did you take my umbrella? I can't find it anywhere!

2. How can you stand that noise I can't!
How can you stand that noise? I can't!

3. The cookies are gone I see only crumbs.
The cookies are gone. I see only crumbs.

4. The dogs were barking they were hungry.
The dogs were barking. They were hungry.

5. She is quite ill please call a doctor immediately!
She is quite ill. Please call a doctor immediately!

6. The clouds came up we knew the storm would hit soon.
The clouds came up. We knew the storm would hit soon.

7. You weren't home he stopped by this morning.
You weren't home. He stopped by this morning.

**57**

---

## Combining Sentences

Some simple sentences can be easily combined into one sentence.

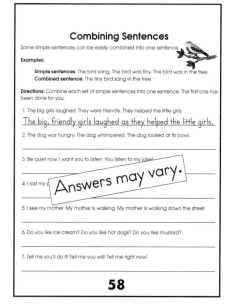

**Examples:**

**Simple sentences:** The bird sang. The bird was tiny. The bird was in the tree.
**Combined sentence:** The tiny bird sang in the tree.

**Directions:** Combine each set of simple sentences into one sentence. The first one has been done for you.

1. The big girls laughed. They were friendly. They helped the little girls.
The big, friendly girls laughed as they helped the little girls.

2. The dog was hungry. The dog whimpered. The dog looked at its bowl.
_____

3. Be quiet now. I want you to listen. You listen to my joke!
_____

4. I lost my p...

Answers may vary.

5. I see my mother. My mother is walking. My mother is walking down the street.
_____

6. Do you like ice cream? Do you like hot dogs? Do you like mustard?
_____

7. Tell me you'll do it! Tell me you will! Tell me right now!
_____

**58**

---

## Punctuation: Commas

Use a comma to separate the number of the day of a month and the year. Do not use a comma to separate the month and year if no day is given.

**Examples:**

June 14, 1999
June 1999

Use a comma after **yes** or **no** when it is the first word in a sentence.

**Examples:**

Yes, I will do it right now.
No, I don't want any.

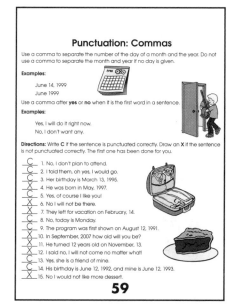

**Directions:** Write **C** if the sentence is punctuated correctly. Draw an **X** if the sentence is not punctuated correctly. The first one has been done for you.

__C__ 1. No, I don't plan to attend.
__C__ 2. I told them, oh yes, I would go.
__C__ 3. Her birthday is March 13, 1995.
__X__ 4. He was born in May, 1997.
__C__ 5. Yes, of course I like you!
__X__ 6. No I will not be there.
__X__ 7. They left for vacation on February, 14.
__X__ 8. No, today is Monday.
__C__ 9. The program was first shown on August 12, 1991.
__X__ 10. In September, 2007 how old will you be?
__X__ 11. He turned 12 years old on November, 13.
__X__ 12. I said no, I will not come no matter what!
__C__ 13. Yes, she is a friend of mine.
__C__ 14. His birthday is June 12, 1992, and mine is June 12, 1993.
__X__ 15. No I would not like more dessert.

**59**

---

## Punctuation: Commas

Use a comma to separate words in a series. A comma is used after each word in a series but is not needed before the last word. Both ways are correct. In your own writing, be consistent about which style you use.

**Examples:**

We ate apples, oranges, and pears.
We ate apples, oranges and pears.

Always use a comma between the name of a city and a state.

**Example:**

She lives in Fresno, California.
He lives in Wilmington, Delaware.

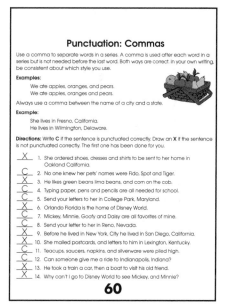

**Directions:** Write **C** if the sentence is punctuated correctly. Draw an **X** if the sentence is not punctuated correctly. The first one has been done for you.

__X__ 1. She ordered shoes, dresses and shirts to be sent to her home in Oakland California.
__C__ 2. No one knew her pets' names were Fido, Spot and Tiger.
__X__ 3. He likes green beans lima beans, and corn on the cob.
__C__ 4. Typing paper, pens and pencils are all needed for school.
__C__ 5. Send your letters to her in College Park, Maryland.
__X__ 6. Orlando Florida is the home of Disney World.
__C__ 7. Mickey, Minnie, Goofy and Daisy are all favorites of mine.
__C__ 8. Send your letter to her in Reno, Nevada.
__X__ 9. Before he lived in New York, City he lived in San Diego, California.
__X__ 10. She mailed postcards, and letters to him in Lexington, Kentucky.
__C__ 11. Teacups, saucers, napkins and silverware were piled high.
__C__ 12. Can someone give me a ride to Indianapolis, Indiana?
__X__ 13. He took a train a car, then a boat to visit his old friend.
__X__ 14. Why can't I go to Disney World to see Mickey, and Minnie?

**60**

---

*English and Grammar: Grade 4*

## Punctuation: Quotation Marks

Use quotation marks (" ") before and after the exact words of a speaker.

**Examples:**

I asked Aunt Martha, "How do you feel?"

"I feel awful," Aunt Martha replied.

Do not put quotation marks around words that report what the speaker said.

**Examples:**

Aunt Martha said she felt awful.

I asked Aunt Martha how she felt.

**Directions:** Write **C** if the sentence is punctuated correctly. Draw an **X** if the sentence is not punctuated correctly. The first one has been done for you.

C 1. "I want it right now!" she demanded angrily.
X 2. "Do you want it now? I asked."
X 3. She said "she felt better" now.
C 4. Her exact words were, "I feel much better now!"
C 5. "I am so thrilled to be here!" he shouted.
C 6. "Yes, I will attend," she replied.
X 7. Elizabeth said "she was unhappy."
C 8. "I'm unhappy," Elizabeth reported.
C 9. "Did you know her mother?" I asked.
X 10. I asked "whether you knew her mother."
C 11. I wondered, "What will dessert be?"
C 12. "Which will it be, salt or pepper?" the waiter asked.
C 13. "No, I don't know the answer!" he snapped.
X 14. He said "yes he'd take her on the trip."
X 15. Be patient, he said. "It will soon be over."

**61**

## Punctuation: Quotation Marks

Use quotation marks around the titles of songs and poems.

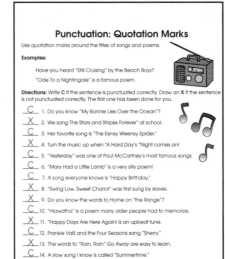

**Examples:**

Have you heard "Still Cruising" by the Beach Boys?

"Ode To a Nightingale" is a famous poem.

**Directions:** Write **C** if the sentence is punctuated correctly. Draw an **X** if the sentence is not punctuated correctly. The first one has been done for you.

C 1. Do you know "My Bonnie Lies Over the Ocean"?
X 2. We sang The Stars and Stripes Forever" at school.
C 3. Her favorite song is "The Eensy Weensy Spider."
X 4. Turn the music up when "A Hard Day's "Night comes on!
C 5. "Yesterday" was one of Paul McCartney's most famous songs.
C 6. "Mary Had a Little Lamb" is a very silly poem!
C 7. A song everyone knows is "Happy Birthday."
X 8. "Swing Low, Sweet Chariot" was first sung by slaves.
X 9. Do you know the words to Home on "the Range"?
C 10. "Hiawatha" is a poem many older people had to memorize.
X 11. "Happy Days Are Here Again! is an upbeat tune.
X 12. Frankie Valli and the Four Seasons sang "Sherry."
X 13. The words to "Rain, Rain" Go Away are easy to learn.
C 14. A slow song I know is called "Summertime."
C 15. Little children like to hear "The Night Before Christmas."

**62**

## Book Titles

All words in the title of a book are underlined. Underlined words also mean italics.

**Examples:**

The Hunt for Red October was a best-seller!
(The Hunt for Red October)

Have you read Lost in Space? (Lost in Space)

**Directions:** Underline the book titles in these sentences. The first one has been done for you.

1. The Dinosaur Poster Book is for eight year olds.
2. Have you read Lion Dancer by Kate Waters?
3. Baby Dinosaurs and Giant Dinosaurs were both written by Peter Dodson.
4. Have you heard of the book That's What Friends Are For by Carol Adorjan?
5. J.B. Stamper wrote a book called The Totally Terrific Valentine Party Book.
6. The teacher read Almost Ten and a Half aloud to our class.
7. Marrying Off Mom is about a girl who tries to get her widowed mother to start dating.
8. The Snow and The Fire are the second and third books by author Caroline Cooney.
9. The title sounds silly, but Goofbang Value Daze really is the name of a book!
10. A book about space exploration is The Day We Walked on the Moon by George Sullivan.
11. Alice and the Birthday Giant tells about a giant who came to a girl's birthday party.
12. A book about a girl who is sad about her father's death is called Rachel and the Upside Down Heart by Eileen Douglas.
13. Two books about baseball are Baseball Bloopers and Oddball Baseball.
14. Katharine Ross wrote Teenage Mutant Ninja Turtles: The Movie Storybook.

**63**

## Book Titles

Capitalize the first and last word of book titles. Capitalize all other words of book titles except short prepositions, such as **of**, **at** and **in**; conjunctions, such as **and**, **or** and **but**; and articles, such as **a**, **an** and **the**.

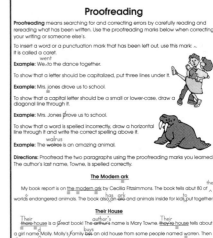

**Examples:**

Have you read War and Peace?

Pippi Longstocking in Moscow is her favorite book.

**Directions:** Underline the book titles. Circle the words that should be capitalized. The first one has been done for you.

1. murder in the blue room by Elliot Roosevelt
2. growing up in a divided society by Sandra Burnham
3. the corn king and the spring queen by Naomi Mitchison
4. new kids on the block by Grace Catalano
5. best friends don't tell lies by Linda Barr
6. turn your kid into a computer genius by Carole Gerber
7. 50 simple things you can do to save the earth by Earth Works Press
8. garfield goes to waist by Jim Davis
9. the hunt for red october by Tom Clancy
10. fall into darkness by Christopher Pike
11. oh the places you'll go by Dr. Seuss
12. amy the dancing bear by Carly Simon
13. the great waldo search by Martin Handford
14. the time and space of uncle albert by Russel Stannard
15. true stories about abraham lincoln by Ruth Gross

**64**

## Proofreading

**Proofreading** means searching for and correcting errors by carefully reading and rereading what has been written. Use the proofreading marks below when correcting your writing or someone else's.

To insert a word or a punctuation mark that has been left out, use this mark: ∧ It is called a caret.
                          went
**Example:** We ∧ to the dance together.

To show that a letter should be capitalized, put three lines under it.

**Example:** Mrs. jones drove us to school.

To show that a capital letter should be a small or lower-case, draw a diagonal line through it.

**Example:** Mrs. Jones Drove us to school.

To show that a word is spelled incorrectly, draw a horizontal line through it and write the correct spelling above it.
          walrus
**Example:** The wolros is an amazing animal.

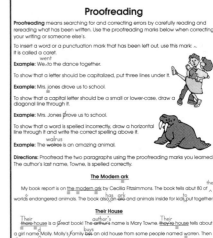

**Directions:** Proofread the two paragraphs using the proofreading marks you learned. The author's last name, Towne, is spelled correctly.

**The Modern ark**                        the
My book report is on the modern ark by Cecilia Fitzsimmons. The book tells abut 80 of
          of                has    ark            to
words endangered animals. The book an are and animals inside for kids put together.

**Their House**
Their                                       author's          Their
there house is a great book! The aurthur's name is Mary Towne. they're house tells about
                               buys
a girl name Molly. Molly's family bys an old house from some people named warren. Then
their
there big problems begin!

**65**

## Proofreading

**Directions:** Proofread the paragraphs, using the proofreading marks you learned. There are seven capitalization errors, three missing words and eleven errors in spelling or word usage.

**Key West**
                a
key West has been tropical paradise ever since
                     famous
Ponce de Leon first saw the set of islands called the
keys in 1513. Two famous streets in Key West are named
                                        cemetery
duval and whitehead. You will find the city sometery
on Francis Street. The tombstones are funny!

The message on one is, "I told you I was sick!"
    a    tombstone       message to
On sailor's tombston is this messge his widow: "At
least know
lease I no where to find him now."
              acres      middle
The cemetery is on 21 akres in the midle of town.

The most famous home in key west is that of the
author                      Hemingway's
auther, Ernest Hemingway. Hemingway's home was
                                    there
at 907 whitehead Street. He lived their for 30 years.

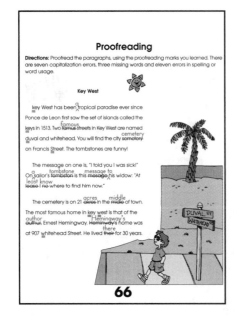

**66**

## Proofreading

**Directions:** Read more about Key West. Proofread and correct the errors. There are eight errors in capitalization, seven misspelled words, a missing comma and three missing words.

**More About Key West**
                   learn
A good way to lern more about key West is to ride the trolley.
                   trolley                          you
Key West has a great troley system. The trolley will take on a tour
                                  see             trolley
of the salt ponds. You can also three red brick forts. The troley tour
                              right
goes by a 110-foot high lighthouse. It is in the middle of the city.
                                              middle
Key west is the only city with a lighthouse in the midle of it! It is also
the southernmost city in the United States.

                  visit
If you have time, the new Ship Wreck Museum. Key west was
          home
also the hom of former president Harry truman. During his
                 Truman
presidency, Truman spent many vacations on key west.

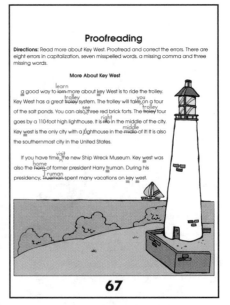

**67**

## Proofreading

**Directions:** Proofread the sentences. Write **C** if the sentence has no errors. Draw an **X** if the sentence contains missing words or other errors. The first one has been done for you.

__C__ 1. The new Ship Wreck Museum in Key West is exciting!

__X__ 2. Another thing I liked was the litehouse.

__C__ 3. Do you remember Hemingway's address in Key West?

__X__ 4. The Key West semetery is on 21 acres of ground.

__X__ 5. Ponce de eon discovered Key West.

__C__ 6. The cemetery in Key West is on Francis Street.

__X__ 7. My favorete tombstone was the sailor's.

__C__ 8. His wife wrote the words on it. Remember?

__X__ 9. The words said, "at least I know where to find him now!"

__C__ 10. That sailor must have been away at sea all the time.

__X__ 11. The troley ride around Key West is very interesting.

__X__ 12. Do you why it is called Key West?

__C__ 13. Can you imagine a lighthouse in the middle of your town?

__X__ 14. It's interesting to no that Key West is our southernmost city.

__C__ 15. Besides Harry Truman and Hemingway, did other famous people live there?

**68**

## Proofreading

**Directions:** Each of the following sentences has a word missing. Use a caret to insert the missing word. The first one has been done for you.

1. Have you ever ridden the trolley around ^Key^ West?

2. The Key West lighthouse ^is^ 110 feet high.

3. Ponce de Leon first ^discovered^ the Keys in 1513.

4. Two famous streets in Key West ^are^ named Duval and Whitehead.

5. The most famous home in Key West ^is^ that of Ernest Hemingway.

6. The cemetery in Key West ^is^ on 21 acres.

7. It is located ^in^ the middle of town.

8. What ^a^ strange place for a cemetery!

9. Many of the tombstones ^are^ funny!

10. The funniest one has ^a^ message from a widow of a sailor.

**69**

# Notes